Adventures in Form

Edited by Tom Chivers

Tom Chivers was born in South London in 1983. His publications include *How To Build A City* (Salt Publishing, 2009), *The Terrors* (Nine Arches Press, 2009; shortlisted for the Michael Marks Award for Poetry Pamphlets) and, as editor, the anthologies *Generation Txt, City State: New London Poetry* and *Stress Fractures: Essays on Poetry* (Penned in the Margins, 2006, 2009 & 2010). A regular reviewer for *Poetry London*, he presented a documentary about the poet Barry MacSweeney for BBC Radio 4 in 2009. He won an Eric Gregory Award in 2011.

Adventures in Form

A Compendium of Poetic Forms, Rules & Constraints

Edited by Tom Chivers

Penned in the Margins

LONDON

PUBLISHED BY PENNED IN THE MARGINS
22 Toynbee Studios, 28 Commercial Street, London E1 6AB, United Kingdom
www.pennedinthemargins.co.uk

Introduction and selection © Tom Chivers
Copyright of the texts rests with the authors

The right of Tom Chivers to be identified as the editor of this work has been asserted
by him in accordance with Section 77 of the Copyright, Designs and Patent Act 1988.

First published 2012

Printed and bound in the UK by Bell & Bain Ltd, Glasgow

ISBN
978-1-908058-01-0

2nd edition

CONTENTS

Adventures in Form

Introduction

The line-break is the most obvious visual characteristic of poetry. It's one of the things most people, I bet, will mention if asked to define a poem. Yet the earliest poetry in the English language – that of the Anglo-Saxons – had no visible line-breaks, but was instead written in continuous blocks of text. After all, why waste good vellum? It was, in effect, prose poetry.

Skip ahead a few centuries, and you'll find some of the earliest examples of 'text speak' in the highly abbreviated Latin of the medieval scriptorium. For instance, 'spiritus sanctus' (The Holy Spirit) might be written s̄p̄s s̄c̄s. With its space-saving contractions and obscure diacritics, this ecclesiastical language was more like code than text; it's tempting to imagine the monkish scribes at home in the Twittersphere. I have always been interested in how the *form* of a piece of writing might be influenced or even determined by the means of its production and/or dissemination, as well as by individual creativity and literary fashion.

In *Adventures in Form*, I hope to show how form can be employed as a framework for innovation. The Oxford English Dictionary defines *adventure* as 'a perilous or audacious undertaking the outcome of which is unknown'; for good use of form should never be predictable.[1] Adventures take you to exotic, faraway places; and I initially envisaged this book as a bestiary of exotic textual creatures: some as strange as the manticore or anthropophagi were to the medieval traveller; others, modified versions of familiar forms.

The *form* of a poem is the deliberate and sustained organisation of

---

[1] The Oxford English Dictionary, www.oed.com, 2011.

visual and aural elements such as line length, metre, rhyme, the distribution of certain letters and sounds, and so on; but can also manifest as its guiding principle, as in the case of a poem which adopts the character of a road sign, a shopping list, or a family tree. A poem's form is distinct from, yet inescapably related to, its content (the *volta* or 'turn' of the sonnet being a good example of this dynamic). As the poet Charlotte Geater put it (writing on my Facebook wall), form is 'what is not said that works for/against what is said'.

Formal poetry (as opposed to form in general) tends to refer to the use of established templates – the villanelle, or the iambic pentameter, say – which impose pre-determined rules regarding metre or rhyme and which, through repeated use, have become codified; in some cases, these forms have come to designate the 'correct' way to write, even to take on specific political or nationalistic connotations (take, for example, the importance of the Ghazal in the artistic identity of Pakistan). In this context, one can understand why some consider free verse to have been a 'liberating' force, unshackling poetry from the weight of literary tradition.

The imposition of form and the desire to escape or reinvent it is, of course, the eternal paradox of art. As Paul Muldoon, has said, 'Form is a straitjacket in the way that a straitjacket was a straitjacket for Houdini.'[2] For a poem is something like an illusionist's trick, and its form describes the organising principles by which this trick is performed. In Muldoon's analogy, form is a kind of willing restraint: an instrument of control wielded by the poem against its author.

As you navigate the fifteen categories of this anthology, you will find that some poets have provided an explanatory note, whilst others have chosen to let the poem speak for itself. This inconsistency reflects the

---

[2] *The Irish Times*, April 19, 2003.

varying degrees to which form makes itself visible in a text. Sometimes we encounter form head-on; and sometimes it is imperceptible, the poem's carefully hidden under-wiring.

Whilst established poetic forms continue to be employed in their thousands, what has caught my attention is the way these hand-me-down templates are being modified, deconstructed and rebuilt in new and exciting ways. I was encouraged to initiate this project by reading *The Reality Street Book of Sonnets*: an extraordinary, cross-generational anthology which approaches one of English literature's most revered forms from a distinctly avant-garde perspective, and which has changed my understanding of the relationship between tradition and experimentation.[3]

Accordingly, the first section in *Adventures of Form*, TRADITIONAL REVISED (p.17) presents a range of brilliantly bastardised sonnets, sestinas and villanelles. Ruth Padel's 'Revelation' is especially intriguing, as it fuses a poetic form, the sonnet, with a biological form, the DNA molecule.

The boundaries of what constitutes a poem have always been porous. FOUND MATERIALS (p.31) introduces the collage poem, a literary form whose progenitor in the visual arts is the surrealist *objet trouvé* (made famous by Marcel Duchamp's *Fountain* of 1917). This section posits the artist not as creator of 'something from nothing', but as arranger or curator of pre-existing texts, often recovered from unexpected situations such as advertising, signage, newspaper headlines or, in the case of Simon Barraclough's poem, the artistic manifesto. The juxtaposition of text and context in the collage can be very funny, as in Chris McCabe's 'Contains Sulphites', which skilfully reclaims the absurd language of parenthood.

The next two sections, DIRECTIONS, INSTRUCTIONS AND POLICY

---

[3] Jeff Hilson, ed., *The Reality Street Book of Sonnets* (Reality Street Editions, 2008).

DOCUMENTS (p.55) and ACADEMIC (p.63), describe, quite loosely, a kind of found poetry in which the form or tone has been lifted from other textual practices, whether bureaucratic, informational or medical. These forms tend especially toward comedy, as in McCabe's 'Submission Policy' or James Wilkes' sequence 'The Review Pages', a surreal parody of the academic review. CORRESPONDENCE (p.67) presents poems written in the form of letters or notes. Direct address to an imagined or real interlocutor can give real momentum to a poem and, as in the case of Patience Agbabi's two sonnets, make space for imaginative satire.

The explosion in mobile, digital technologies and social networking in the early twenty-first century provides new opportunities for poetic form. TXTS, TWEETS AND STATUS UPDATES (p.81) captures such experiments in short form, and offers a creative rebuttal to those who blame 'text speak' for declining standards of written English. In the text poems of George Ttoouli and Hannah Silva, language often appears damaged or distorted, generating that sense of defamiliarisation – of 'making strange' – that is one of poetry's principle qualities, but which is more often located in the site of metaphor.

Nathan Penlington's 'unpredictive' is an interactive poem; it provides us with only a numerical code, asking the reader to decipher the text. Nathan and I deliberated the inclusion of this poem, as its deciphering requires access to software now made obsolete by smartphones. But I hope this will send readers scrabbling around in the attic for old handsets.

The poems in SITES OF EROSION (p.95) enact various methods of reduction. Whilst reduction is arguably the natural state of poetry – it being already a condensed form of expression – the poem rarely incorporates the actual process of erasure into its own text, as occurs in these examples. The exception here is Sam Riviere's 'Austerities' sequence, where the precise form is looser and not immediately visible, but the impulse to reduce no less urgent. His approach, writing in response to government funding cuts, 'deprive[s] the poems of formal characteristics, typical sentiments and subjects, by acting out a kind of hostility towards poetry.'

The primary objective of a translation is usually to transfer the *sense* of an original text from one language to another. The poems in TRANSLATIONS AND VERSIONS (p.105) explore more unorthodox strategies, applying formal methods concerned with a text's aural or visual elements, or which introduce randomness/automation into the translation process. They ask us to consider the differences between inspiration, originality and creative plagiarism, the author proposed as a collaborator working with a source text.

N+7 (p.119) and UNIVOCALIST (p.129) showcase two such strategies or *constraints*, both creations of the French post-/anti-surrealist writing group Oulipo, whose practices are experiencing a revival of interest in modern British poetry. N+7 is a translation process in which each noun in the original text is replaced by the seventh noun after it in the dictionary (the results vary depending on the length of your dictionary). Ross Sutherland's translation of Little Red Riding Hood is one of the best examples of the form, although he had to look a little further than seven places: 'The Liverish Red-Blooded Riffraff Hoo-ha' is written using N+23. The Univocalism is a poem written using only one vowel, whose consequent musicality lends itself particularly to performance and comedy.

EMERGENT (p.135) takes its name from Edwin Morgan's description of a concrete poem in which one text appears to *emerge* from another, often by breaking the poem down into its constituent words, phonemes and/or letters, and rearranging them into a dense pattern. The effects of these poems are startlingly visual and musical, assuming the quality of a mantra. Paul Muldoon's 'Eating Chinese Food in a Straw Bale House, Snowmass, Colorado, January 2011' is one of several poems in this book which employ unorthodox typography (others include Roddy Lumsden's time-splice poem and Ira Lightman's 'Worduko'). I am keen to emphasise the visual possibilities of form, but considering this project's already-wide scope, decided to avoid fully embracing concrete poetry; that meeting point of text, type and visual art which has developed into a distinct artform of its own.

A newer phenomenon that extends the possibilities of the poem is 'internet poetry', where the forms (memes, screenshots, multimedia collages) echo and comment on the rapid proliferation of content online. They exploit absurd, ironic and wildly inappropriate juxtapositions, feeding a mash-up culture where everything can be hacked. As Theodoros Chiotis has noted, 'digital poetry splices together informational spaces'.[4] Theo has contributed one of his own innovative poems to CODE IS POETRY (p.143). The title of this short section is a well-known programming adage – one I've been keen on ever since I taught myself to write BASIC and HTML code in the mid 90s. Poetry and computer code do have a lot in common: syntax, semantics, economy of expression. Both can be somewhat esoteric, and depend on their success on the precise placement of a word, letter or symbol.

The use of digital and scientific technology in generating writing challenges Coleridge's notion of poetry as 'purely human'[5]. The author becomes a co-author, open to random acts outside his or her control. In NUMEROLOGY (p.147) Valerie Laws' 'Quantum Sheep' demonstrates the poem as a scientific experiment whose outcome is unknown. Other poems in this section borrow mathematical structures from the Fibonacci sequence and the football pitch.

Whilst writers and publishers often grumble about poetry's marginality, a love of language and wordplay continues to express itself throughout popular culture in crosswords, puzzles – even the British

---

[4] Theodoros Chiotis, 'These Terabytes I Have Tried to Shore Agaiainst Our Ruins', in Tom Chivers, ed., *Stress Fractures: Essays on Poetry* (Penned in the Margins, 2010).
[5] Samuel Taylor Coleridge, 'On Poesy and Art' (1818).

obsession with the pun. The playful poems in WORD GAMES (p.155) make use of collective nouns, anagrams, Scrabble and Sudoku. Here poetic form becomes, in the words of Jon Stone (again, writing on Facebook), 'a playground climbing frame'.

The final section of this book, AND OTHER INVENTIONS (p.161), is partly inspired by the Scottish poet and editor Roddy Lumsden. Roddy is a serial inventor of new forms, with names like the Sevenling, the Hebdomad and the Ripple Poem. These forms combine linguistic playfulness with the obsessiveness of the puzzle writer (Roddy is a trivia buff and has worked as a puzzle and quiz writer). Perhaps in ten or fifty years time, the Wilson, the Sudo and the Yvette Carte-Blanche will be as popular as the haiku and pantoum are now. After all, every form must start somewhere.

Form is not something merely to be ignored as irrelevant and old-fashioned or, conversely, defended at all costs against the barbarians of free verse. In any vital literary culture, form must be subject to repeated renewal. In showcasing a wide, though far from exhaustive, range of new forms, this anthology speaks, I hope, to the enduring biodiversity of contemporary poetry. If form is, as *The Oxford Dictionary of Literary Terms* defines it, a 'critical term with a confusing variety of meanings', then this collection embraces that variety and celebrates confusion.[6]

Tom Chivers
London, February 2012

---

[6] www.oxfordreferenceonline.com

TRADITIONAL REVISED

Once
Colette Bryce

Some words you may use only once.
Repeat them to some newer heart
and all your accuracy is gone.

Sweetheart, Darling. Years on,
how the old terms fail;
words that we loved with, once.

Older, on our second chance,
we stand, faltering hearts
in hands, inaccurate

and passionate, in love's
late, unfurnished rooms,
full of the words we cannot use;

and drive home, the same
streets, drop through the gears
to steer around the gone

words, the known
words, the beautiful outworn
words, those we may use only once,
all our accuracy gone.

Hello my friend

HANNAH SILVA

I am contacting you with something urgent,
you have always been a good friend.
I need to inform you of the following:
It is important that we remain connected.
It is important we don't avoid the subject.
Please switch on your TV and watch the news.

Nothing happens in the world that isn't in the news,
nothing happens in the news that isn't urgent,
nothing happens until there is an urgent subject
and I would not be contacting you my friend
if it wasn't for the importance of remaining connected,
if it wasn't that so many are following.

There is perhaps something sinister about following
with such attentiveness the many faces of the news.
Sometimes I wonder if we really need to be connected
to an idea, a chink in history that only now is urgent.
I wonder why I feel the need for a friend
when friendship has become a meaningless subject.

Yet I am asking you to stand alongside me on the subject,
I ask you to confess that we have been following
the instructions of a face we both called a friend
and I ask you to smile with me as we state that the news

of this latest update is a shock and that retraction is urgent
and we celebrate the fact that minds have connected.

There was a time when people became connected
when we connected them, became subject
when we subjected them, their ideas were never urgent
until we believed them. They followed and kept following,
we told our stories and our stories became news.
Keep dancing and you will always have a friend.

I understand the world through faces I call friends,
every day I ensure to remain connected.
There are many sources from which I glean news
in the space above my thoughts I leave 'no subject'.
There are hundreds of people who are following
my brief statements and their replies are always urgent.

Hello my dear friend there is no subject no winning numbers
I am keeping you connected and I am following you
I've told you the good news and now await your urgent respond.

A sestina whose *envoi* (repeated phrase) is from spam emails.

Revelation

RUTH PADEL

'A ladder,' the master whispered, 'of nucleic acid.'
This was the first we'd heard of it.
Rain nosed the glass; wind lashed the trees
outside. 'Four hydrogen-bonded nucleotides
locking on like mating damsel flies. But each
a different size, pulling the ladder's sides
into a twirl, like serpents on the sign
outside a chemist who, for old time's sake,
gives lodging in his window to the alchemist's
glass jars.' He drew those twinned snakes
looping up the wand
of God-Who-Escorts-Our-Morphia-Laden-Dead
to forest mist and shadowlands, where they belong,
and brings them back in dreams.
'But one snake, the lagging strand,
is upside down.' A squeak of chalk.
The pavilion, I recall, was dark.
Rain pooled on the *mesua* floor.
'We're conflict from the start. One thread
runs easy, the other's fitful. Broken tickertape
on which genetic script, your soul's barcode,
emerges opposite.' What did we know?
We longed for a match, a cell phone, anything
that glowed. 'As in a mirror, messages
are written here and must be read

backwards.' We waited for the prayer
that never came. '*Otherwise* is built in.
Behold your molecule of heredity.
Two cosmic serpents, yes; but tail to head.'

┌ ┐
This poem is a double-sonnet, stuck together with a single line in the
middle. It is inspired by the structure of the DNA molecule and the central
line starts the theme of the backwards-running strand of the molecule.
└ ┘

Nausea

Tim Turnbull

Guns will make us nervous. Butter will only make us sick.
Rerun the Pathe newsreels of ideologues in horn-rimmed specs;

where vicious, half-wit colonels brandish Mausers for effect.
Show acid-addled demagogues in grainy teevee clips,

preaching personal fulfillment and foretelling the apocalypse
or media mogul robber-barons urging the people to elect

a stiletto wielding psycho who inspires fear but no respect,
ailing pontiffs, left-wing mayors and plutocrats with walking sticks

and package them and put them on in one extended telethon.
Ensure it's shown around the world, in every bar, in every home,

through cable and by satellite beamed into everybody's lives
until it's unremarkable, a commonplace as the moon and the sun.

Make us watch it till we're numb. Make us watch it till we groan,
Guns will make us break down crying, butter bring us out in hives.

⌐ A breakbeat sonnet. ⌐

Inch & Co Cash Chemists

Tamar Yoseloff

The stench of hash met his nose,
cocaine-catch in his chest. He hitched
the hem of his moth-ash coat, stashed
the mess – a case of cats & mice.

A mash on the chin, a stitch – a Scotch
to thin the ache. Once he tossed a coin –
China or Cheam; an itch in the mists
of time. He missed the hit, the scent

of sin, the chime of cents. Same shit –
the *can't* of cant, the stain of shame.
The months aim mace at him. That's it,
in the can. Do the maths – he's mince.

Me, I'm chaste, I'm sane.
I am his chain, his match.

> An Oulipo-inspired sonnet in which the letters of the title are used to form
> the words in the poem (excepting prepositions).

Capacity

TAMAR YOSELOFF

Fat chance you'll ever break out of here,
this depository for great mistakes
you've made your home. Just enough room
for a bed and a stool, a cell of sorts,
for a man of thin means. Lean times.
But I'm a girl who's capable
and culpable, who knows the value
of a pound. You can't resist the give
of my carapace, my caterpillar lips,
my capacious thighs. I'll never sell you
short. You'll never let me down.
For the first time, you are full
to the very brim with the milk
of human kindness. Moo.

Duk of   gton

TAMAR YOSELOFF

Gone, the days of ho fun duck,
back of the truck fooling around,
white guy funk, goon squad drunks,
a ton of laughs. I nearly puked.
Forgotten in the glummy dusk,
a glutton for a punch up. Fuck it.
I'm done with doom, dark core
of nothing, morning lost, the *ack ack*
of a crow on a branch, same old,
same old. Don't even know what's
missing, though there's a hole
in my heart, an ache in my brain,
a pandora's trunk of trouble,
and no one to open me up.

Flat Iron Square

TAMAR YOSELOFF

No *you are here* to show you where:
ass-end of nowhere, you are square
off the map, circling your steps
like a dog tracking a trail of piss.
A curse, a rasp, a chokedamp cough,
a stifled laugh. Their faces graze
the faded smiles of plywood – little kids
with thumbs for eyes, skin clingfilmed
over bones, mouths wide as caves:
you look as if you've seen a ghost.
What a waste, your lousy life, your
flat-iron face. The corners curling
with boredom. Now you're one of them,
a stooge in the room, a stench.

These sonnets are from a sequence informed by photographs of urban
signage / ghost signs. The sonnets are informal and their narratives
fragmented to reflect the ruined atmosphere of their subjects. Each sonnet
plays linguistic and thematic games with its title and location.

Talula-Does-The-Hula-From-Hawaii

Kirsten Irving

Where do stupid names end up, these shorn tags
tied on toes by parents with the abandon
and foresight of tyrants annoying their court?

Today the three of you, now strangers, leave court
in opposite directions, untying cloakroom tags
from belongings, as you abandon

what passed for a name. That punchline abandoned
to the playground's corrupt court
and the toilet wall's smeared tags.

Tags abandoned, a girl who's not Talula courts the world.


```
┌                                                  ┐
   A Tritina (a shorter version of the Sestina)
└                                                  ┘
```

A Volta for the Sonnet as a Drag Queen

Sophie Mayer

1

The sonnet's a drag, and girl, it knows: sticks its
falsies, lines up its lashes. Lamé, lurex, tits
aglitter, it plays the crying game. To be real.
To see how it makes you, makes you, makes you feel,

to be real. The sonnet's a pose. Vogue. Let your
body be told what (not) to do. To the letter,
in its frame. Again, again. Limbs aglow/akimbo
if enjambed: the stance, the torch, the blow

that's always coming. The twist, you know it.
What's underneath the hood. In her panties.
What reveals, conceals. What (split) ends. Take no shit,
darling, that's the deal. The impossible with ease.

2

This ooze is us: the tilting city of us visible
in its shunting, in its melismas. Who cast us
in clear resin, jarred us, until here we are: dis
played. Mutated to meet the needs of
a poisoned world. Gill to gill we dance,
my crotch pressed up between your prostheses,
the necklace of my tumours tangled
in your iridescent locks. What prophetic tango
our skin speaks, our nifty six fingertips (light
at loom or touchscreen, equally). My squally
darling, my freak show embryo: we will drag
ourselves over the slivers. Spike our cha-cha heels
with them, rim each orifice with shards of glass.
And glitter. And glitter. And. And glitter.

> This poem combines a down-the-line sonnet highlighting form as drag with
> an exploded (cancerous, mutated) sonnet.

FOUND MATERIALS

O Manifest

Simon Barraclough

O mother of a ditch, brimful with muddy water!
Down with all marble-chippers who are cluttering up our squares.
It is the monotony of the nude against which we fight.
I'd like the artist to forget that he's Japanese,
to liberate Venice from the whorish moonlight of its furnished
                                                bedrooms
the way a surgeon dissects a corpse.
We are at the beginning of a springtime;
it is the painful joy of wounded flesh, the joyous pain of a
                                                flowering.
The future is behind us.
It is useful to put manure on barren ground
but this dirty work does not interest us.
We must invent hap-hap-hap-hap-happy clothes, daring clothes,
for the smallest people live in the greatest houses.
The eye only sees what the spirit draws its attention to.
The masterpiece must die with its author.
The English character is based on the sea,
the present can be intensely sentimental.

This is the supreme imbecility of your confidence
in economic legislation, vice-crusades and uniform education.
Distortion is an altimeter crammed with wrinkles and grey hair
and this is torture worse than breaking on the wheel
till one goes crazy. Till one loses consciousness.
Our time is one of metal, it continues to spit
out a fountain of stagnant water.

This poem, part of a growing manifesto, contains 24 lines from 24 artistic manifestos. See *100 Artists' Manifestos: From the Futurists to the Stuckists*, edited by Alex Danchev (Penguin Modern Classics, 2011).

Signs & Shivers

Iain Sinclair

BEACH SOCCER AXED OVER GUN VIOLENCE
FOX SAVAGES BABY TWINS
MOLEMAN TUNNELLER FOUND DEAD

DRIVING BAN DAD HANGED HIMSELF
SEX SPY 'CHARMED' GAZETTE SNAPPER

ECO-MUSLIM & FORMER PRESENTER
WIN GREAT TRIP TO SOUTH AFRICA
JUDGE STICKS KNIFE IN HACKNEY

QUEEN'S OFFICIAL BIRTHDAY
(SUBJECT TO CONFIRMATION)

WORLD'S TALLEST MAN
RETRIEVES OBJECT
FROM SICK DOLPHIN

FOX IN BLINDMAN'S BEDROOM
DEAF CAT IN MOTORWAY HORROR
LOST FRENCH TRUCKER KILLED OAP

EX-SOLDIER BEAT PAL INTO COMA
CUT CRIME WITH FEWER POLICE

FIREBUGS TORCH PARK AVIARY
A SHORT ROUTE TO A LONG BOX

U-TURN OVER GIANT BUNNY MURAL
CANNIBAL COPS FIND KILLER'S KIT

GIVE ME A CIGAR & RAISE THE SHADES

The Analogue Guide to Parenting

CHRIS MCCABE

Day 1

Why have you chewed the monkey?
Don't push the lion in the postbox.
Careful on the pony with a full nappy.
Why have you chewed the monkey?
Don't get jam in the ridges.
Why have you chewed the monkey?

You've scrawled ink everywhere now it's time for books.
Now the bus is in the hollandaise.
I was trying to educate you then but forget it.
Now the bus is in the hollandaise.
We're not made of toast.
Why have you chewed the monkey?

Naughty boys don't go on swings.
Don't push the lion in the postbox.
Why have you chewed the monkey?
Why have you chewed the monkey?
I was trying to educate you then but forget it.
You can only have your milk if you're going to sleep.

You've scrawled ink everywhere now it's time for books.
Don't push the lion in the postbox.

Naughty boys don't go on swings.
I was trying to educate you then but forget it.
You can only have your milk if you're going to sleep.
Careful on the pony with a full nappy.

Day 3

Naughty boys don't go on swings.
We're not made of toast.
Now the bus is in the hollandaise.
I was trying to educate you then but forget it.
Naughty boys don't go on swings.
I was trying to educate you then but forget it.

Careful on the pony with a full nappy.
Watch the ark across the oak.
Naughty boys don't go on swings.
You've scrawled ink everywhere now it's time for books.
You've scrawled ink everywhere now it's time for books.
You've scrawled ink everywhere now it's time for books.

Why have you chewed the monkey?
Now the bus is in the hollandaise.
Don't push the lion in the postbox.
We're not made of toast.
Don't get jam in the ridges.
Now the bus is in the hollandaise.

Now the bus is in the hollandaise.
Careful on the pony with a full nappy.
Watch the ark across the oak.
To have more fun you need to go higher.
Careful on the pony with a full nappy.
Why have you chewed the monkey?

Day 5

Why have you chewed the monkey?
Why have you chewed the monkey?
Watch the ark across the oak.
Don't get jam in the ridges.
You can only have your milk if you're going to sleep.
Naughty boys don't go on swings.

To have more fun you need to go higher.
Don't get jam in the ridges.
Careful on the pony with a full nappy.
Why have you chewed the monkey?
Watch the ark across the oak.
You've scrawled ink everywhere now it's time for books.

Now the bus is in the hollandaise.
To have more fun you need to go higher.
Don't push the lion in the postbox.
Now the bus is in the hollandaise.
To have more fun you need to go higher.

You've scrawled ink everywhere now it's time for books.

Don't push the lion in the postbox.
Don't push the lion in the postbox.
Careful on the pony with a full nappy.
Don't push the lion in the postbox.
Now the bus is in the hollandaise.
Watch the ark across the oak.

Day 7

Don't push the lion in the postbox.
You've scrawled ink everywhere now it's time for books.
You can only have your milk if you're going to sleep.
Naughty boys don't go on swings.
Careful on the pony with a full nappy.
We're not made of toast.

I was trying to educate you then but forget it.
Don't get jam in the ridges.
We're not made of toast.
Don't push the lion in the postbox.
Watch the ark across the oak.
Don't get jam in the ridges.

Watch the ark across the oak.
Naughty boys don't go on swings.
I was trying to educate you then but forget it.

Now the bus is in the hollandaise.
You've scrawled ink everywhere now it's time for books.
Why have you chewed the monkey?

Don't get jam in the ridges.
We're not made of toast.
Now the bus is in the hollandaise.
Don't push the lion in the postbox.
Naughty boys don't go on swings.
To have more fun you need to go higher.

Influenced by Jackson MacLow's approach to his Daily Life poems, this poem was made by creating a 'seed text' and then arranging the lines through a random element. I was becoming alarmed at the amount of inane statements parenthood was making me speak. To get some distance from this I wrote down the next 12 inane parenting comments I made. At the time Pavel loved to be held up to the clock and to randomly point at the numbers with a pen. To create the poem I numbered each of my inane comments 1-12 and then held Pavel up to the clock to randomly point at the numbers 1-12. As each number corresponded to one of my lines I generated a poem from the lines based on this random sequencing. I did this 24 times to represent one day in my life as a parent. I then did this 7 more times to create a week in my life as a parent.

Voices of the Dead

STEVE SPENCE

Knowing how to feel is more important than what you feel.
This surely depends less on the robots than on the quality of
the humans who design them. Should beauty be painted with
her head in the clouds? She still has occasional mood swings
but they're nowhere near as severe. From the water everything
looks different yet most learning happens casually and without
programmed instruction. A system of uncertainty has entered
our daily lives. Pollack like a slow-moving bait and for that
reason the action of your rubber eel is important. As mutinies
go this is a very laid-back affair. Some scientists say that our
planet is running out of platinum. This may or may not be
true but every cloud has its moment in the sun. During the manic
phase there can be feelings of inflated self-esteem verging on
grandiosity. Do you have the ability to spot the next big thing?

Austerity rules, okay!

STEVE SPENCE

I have been here too long but I have yet to find a
suitable guide who can guess where I am going.
Cash remains the most important method of payment
for small transactions yet their manifesto promises
to maintain current levels of defence spending.
Successful applicants will be required to provide
an enhanced disclosure. It is low tide and directly
below the doorway the shore lies exposed. Fifteen
miles off the coast a sea turtle is seen struggling
through the slick. Coral reefs in many parts of the
world now face devastation yet she is as trendily
crisp and flawlessly groomed as you might expect.
To qualify, simply switch to our high interest
account using our hassle-free switching service.

> The method used to produce these poems is a mix of chance and of using
> varied material with related/unrelated themes to give the impression
> of continuous flow, even if this flow is abruptly interrupted at times. I
> have taken extracts from a wide variety of sources, played with them
> sometimes, creating unexpected juxtapostions. I have in mind The Clock
> by Christian Marclay, a film which lasts for 24 hours and can be recycled in
> a loop, to be viewed in perpetuity.

There is an Epigraph

CHRISSY WILLIAMS

"Gather ye rosebuds while ye may"
> *To the Virgins, to make much of Time*
> Robert Herrick

"Every night I cut out my heart,
but in the morning it was full again."
> Count Almásy, *The English Patient*
> Michael Ondaatje

"I like my evil like I like my men — evil."
> Buffy Summers, *Buffy the Vampire Slayer 4:9 'Pangs'*
> Joss Whedon

"Realize that the grieving process will not take forever.
Time will eventually feel [sic] all wounds including this death."
> *How to Mourn the Death of a Dog*, eHow.com
> luyoung

"I see dead people."
> Cole Sear, *The Sixth Sense*
> M. Night Shyamalan

> The classic epigrapha consists of five epigraphs from different sources whose placement remove the need for any subsequent poem.

The Briefing

PAUL STEPHENSON

It will be the year hot water bottles went glam.
Boxy and bright jackets will just make the edit,
some fire-engine red, some twice double-breasted.
Things will very nearly go wrong more quickly
than you can say 'We need to talk about Kevin'.

Luckily, the actor will follow his lead closely, busting
out some floor-length tricks with a look made up
partly of separates, adding no unnecessary fluff or jazzle.
The combo to explore will be blue and chocolate.
Gorge dresses will be launched in another Celine-ism.

There'll be a smashing pea coat, which, unlike the bulk
does not feature the eagle icon. Classy decision will extend
across the smart blazers too. Elsewhere the line will be
relaunched to older, very this-year crowds. People
will exit galleries and go to the previous page. Arrows

left and right, party-centric earrings to fall in love with
and parkas getting a colour boost. Aside swirly whirlers,
hints of lace at the neck, power oozing in the reek
of 1980. The hottest word about town will be peplum.
People won't feel the shoes but it's a small quibble.

Beeswax-cotton hanging labels will fire on all cylinders,
collaborating with interior blogger antikmodern
lounge chairs with stripes for forward-reading.
When the capsule collection of chokers hits the high,
brooches of verve will glitz the one-off trunk with tucking.

This poem is composed entirely of descriptions of garments from the
fashion pages of *The Guardian*.

Family Values
Paul Stephenson

I thought it would be this kind of crescendo moment, but it wasn't.
We just ate over-boiled vegetables and my mother cried and cried;
she hadn't realised the giblets were plastic-bagged inside.

I grew up hand-to-mouth, dancing on egg and chips in North Wales,
but couldn't be more pleased how my children have turned out.

My eldest is 19 and adored by everybody. She's very, very clever,
plans to be a particle physicist, regularly whoops about anti-matter.

The youngest wants to be a stand-up comedian or wigged barrister,
has a natural talent for jokes and coming up with a pack of lies.

I'll encourage them to do whatever they desire, but either way they'll
follow in my footsteps. They appreciate everything and expect nothing.

Their grandfather was a big belly-laugher. I laugh too. Asian families,
Italian families do it, that's the norm. Our way was not the norm.
I can still smell that chicken and cherish my foraged wishbone.

A reworking of a short biograpy of Carol Vorderman, former Channel 4
'Countdown' presenter and mathematical whizz, in *The Guardian*.

The Protagonist

PAUL STEPHENSON

You'll remember him well as the manipulative tabby with disembodied voice, a bona fide weirdo unfurling flashbacks and over-reactions. What face work! Rush to see him without wrapping pour honey onto toast from a vial (no, it's not technically a test tube), then tongue the long-lost moment, lick it burn-resistant. Put simply, he's the essential difference between what you see and what you get, out 'n' about scalpelling global hides, scrubbing striped monsters in plushest villas. He excises all duties, his custom to make a drop of blood bloom casually like a rose garden, into a madding playground, a heavy-scented scar park. You're not convinced?

Listen! This man shoos his menagerie of crazies frequently, no time to swan around taking prisoners carving endings into their own neck. A clip-board controller of destinies, subtle inside a tiger costume or visual in-joke, those incarcerated eyes are his signature give-away. Probing deep into welling entrails, he's attractive and welcome to prettiness, subtitled dizziness, v. v. unstable but smorgasbord gorgeous. Mayhem's a safe bet in his narrative arc. He'll rework you loosely, the public gazing on as your beachfront melts.

> This poem was written by crashing and colliding text, deleting words to create new meanings through the juxtaposition of unexpected - and unintended - neighbouring words. It is from a *Guardian* review of Pedro Almódovar's film *The Skin I Live In*.

Notes on Contributors
PAUL STEPHENSON

Alison was born
Brian grew up

Chloe is a full-time
Dan devotes his spare

Eliza took part
Fabian has been a member

Gill divides her
Henry is completing

Isabel was a stand-up
Joel once sat on

Kirsten is currently
Lars was an inner-city

Marion lives between
Nick is now

Olga was the first
Pablo continues to

Quinn chairs
River runs

Saskia often gives
Tod recently received

Uma submitted
Victor used to

Wendy was highly
Xavier appears often

Yolanda emphasizes
Zach will be.

This poem collages the beginnings of biographical notes from the back
of poetry magazines. Some mags feature contributor notes, others
don't, deeming them irrelevant, or else detracting from the poems. I am
fascinated by how writers choose to sum themselves up in two or three
lines. These couplets create oppositions, some of which, with the object
of the sentence omitted, result in rather suggestive entries.

Christina Lindberg: A Collage

JON STONE

When waiting and wanting aren't enough,
you'll see scenes of a girl – young, frightening,
growing up. Previously only whispered about.

She's not a little girl anymore. She has
new interests, her own terrible kind of body.
You've seen her in 23 nightmares,

alone on a motion picture screen, everything
there is to know about love. Her nudity
is a weekend you are urged not to attend.

Her speech is unpromotable, a film
of feeling and sexual activity. If you are
embarrassed, put on a new awareness.

Forget revenge and the hard, naked truth.
She has so much to give: mercy, cruelty,
beauty that would make a shambles of you.

In the clutches of her, disaster is experience,
Stockholm a penthouse, the 1970s innocent.
There has never been another coming.

When waiting and wanting aren't enough,

you'll see what was left of every blow,
every cut. Shameful, you'll see all of her.

Collaged from the trailers for *The Depraved, Maid in Sweden* and *They Call Her One Eye.*

Alistair MacLean's Death Train

JON STONE

"It is hoped that the publication of Death Train, *and of further novels based on MacLean outlines, will please the many readers for whom Alistair MacLean's death has left a gap. Certainly MacLean fans will find that* Death Train ... *has all the action and suspense for which Alistair MacLean was renowned."*

Flung hundreds of feet in the air, landing in the snow-laced
predicament, she smiled to herself when trying to think.
"Balashika," Kolchinsky whispered, ashen-faced.
First the rotors, then the fuselage of a Lynx
entered the compartment and slid the door shut.
Kolchinsky gripped the proffered hand
and unbuttoned his cashmere overcoat.
A light snow had fallen over Central Switzerland
where the train came to a halt,
which was subsequently proved to have been an accident.
He fumbled to unclip the keys from his belt,
the conductor's look of bewilderment
from years of neglect. It was the only way in.
You have thirty seconds to throw down your gun.

You Wave Me

CHRISSY WILLIAMS

SIDE A

Baby, I Love You	Aretha Franklin 2:38
Love Will Tear Us Apart	Joy Division 3:26
Chase The Tear	Portishead 5:15
Cut To The Chase	Morcheeba 4:20
A Chicken With Its Head Cut Off	The Magnetic Fields 2:42
Drunk Chicken/America	U2, Allen Ginsberg 1:31
Too Drunk To Fuck	Dead Kennedys 2:41
Fuck the Pain Away	Peaches 4:10
Sail Away	The Rapture 5:21
Sailor Song	Regina Spektor 3:15
Repression Song	Hefner 2:52
Turkey And Repression	Noam Chomsky 2:06
Turkey Mambo Momma	Pulp 2:54

SIDE B

I Love To Mambo	Billy Taylor Trio 2:57
Crazy In Love	Beyoncé feat. Jay-Z 3:56
My Wife's Crazy!	David Cross 3:52
My Wife, Lost In The World	Beirut 3:13
Lost Not Found	Dirty Vegas 4:06
Natural's Not In It	Gang of Four 3:06
Only In It For The $$$	The Shivers 4:16
Money (Edit)	The Flying Lizards 2:33
Brain Editing	Khoiba 3:28
Insane In The Brain	Cypress Hill 3:27
A Short Reprise For Mary Todd, Who Went Insane,	
But For Very Good Reasons	Sufjan Stevens 0:47
Reasons To Be Cheerful (Part 3)	Ian Dury, The Blockheads 4:45
A Cheery Wave From Stranded Youngsters	Mogwai 2:18
Wish Me Luck (As You Wave Me Goodbye)	Vera Lynn 3:10

⌐   ¬

A Poemixtape. One word must link each song title to the next. Two sides
required, max. 45 mins each. Playlists available on Spotify: Poem as
Mixtape - side A and Poem as Mixtape - side B.

DIRECTIONS, INSTRUCTIONS AND POLICY DOCUMENTS

Directions
INUA ELLAMS

After Billy Collins

You know the wild bush at the back of the flat,
the one that scrapes the kitchen window
the one that struggles for soil and water,
and fails where the train tracks scar the ground?
And you know how if you leave the bush
and walk the stunted land you come
to crossroads, paved just weeks ago:
hot tar over the flattened roots of trees,
and a squad of traffic lights, red-eyed now
stiff against the filth stained fallen leaves?

And farther on, you know
the bruised allotments with the broken sheds
and if you go beyond that you hit
the first block of Thomas Street Estate?
Well, if you enter and ascend, and you

might need a running jump over
dank puddles into the shaking lift
that goes no further than the fourth floor,
you will eventually come to a rough rise
of stairs that reach without railings
the run-down roof as high as you can go
and a good place to stop.

The best time is late evening
when the moon fights through
drifts of fumes as you are walking,
and when you find an upturned bin
to sit on, you will be able to see
the smog pour across the city
and blur the shapes and tones
of things and you will be attacked
by the symphony of tires, airplanes,
sirens, screams, engines
and if this is your day you might even
catch a car chase or a hear a horde
of biker boys thunder-cross a bridge.

But it is tough to speak these things
how tufts of smog enter the body
and begin to wind us down
how the city chokes us painfully against
its chest made of secrets and fire
how we, built of weaker things regard
our sculpted landscape, water flowing

through pipes, the clicks of satellites
passing over clouds and the roofs
where we stand in the shudder of progress
giving ourselves to the vast outsides.

Still, text me before you set out.
Knock when you reach my door
and I will walk you as far as the tracks
with water for your travels and a hug.
I will watch after you and not turn back
to the flat till you merge
with the throngs of buses and cyclists,
heading down toward the block,
scuffing the ground with your feet.

Submission Policy
CHRIS MCCABE

Please send no more than four gnomes

There is a cost of five peonies for entering each gnome

Gnomes must be accompanied by an SAE no bigger than the gnomes themselves

If you don't believe passionately in your gnomes how can you expect us to?

Gnomes must be no taller than 49 lines

Accompany your gnomes with a concise biography

All winning gnomes will be asked to a prizewinning event where they'll be asked to give a short reading

Gnomes must be original and previously unseen elsewhere

The warning signs we should have made

HANNAH JANE WALKER & CHRIS THORPE

In the case of fire, do not have sex in this lift.
Do not use your lanyard as a noose, even when jesting.
Do not scratch your eczema over the biscuit tin.
The CCTV in the toilets is not an invitation to a display of piss
                                                        athletics.
Do not smoke near the accounts marked flammable,
unless you have been expressly told to do so.
Danger, high voltage, does not recharge your iPhone super
                                                        quickly,
the spillage in the foyer is not an ice rink,
do not hold up cards marking falls out of 10.
Please do not stand on office swivel chairs. Just don't.
In the interests of hygiene, please wash your hands,
mind the step, keep the fire door shut,
do not run your genitals under the tap that says caution, very hot
                                                        water.
Do not photocopy the stairs,
do not do monkey impressions from the panic bar,
in fact do not touch the panic bar,
do not even think about touching the panic bar.
Do not use social media to give the manager your diagnosis,
and do not put your fingers in the water cooler to wind up the
                                                        piranhas.
Above all, do not ignore these warnings.

When shooting stray dogs at the abandoned nuclear plant
do not pick up pebbles to take home as souvenirs.
They may be contaminated with radioactive material
and therefore dangerous to you and your family.
This automobile is not designed for certain pastimes.
It is not safe to attempt fellatio while driving,
impacts sustained at speed during oro-genital activity
may cause the sudden amputation of the penis.

These are the warning signs we should have made.
For the Oh Fuck Moments we had not imagined.
Some things we never know until they happen.
But second guessing them would mean more sign than planet.

MEDICAL QUESTIONNAIRE
STRICTLY CONFIDENTIAL
JAMES WILKES

State if you have suffered from any of the following:

Tuberculosis	NO
A detached voice	YES/NO
Fainting or Migraine	YES/NO
Blood coughing	NO
Proper names	NO
Compulsion to invent devices	YES/NO
Coughing or hoarseness	YES/NO
Sciatica, of long duration	NO
An unholy din	YES/NO
An empire of crime	YES

Is any investigation pending? If so please specify I LOST MY VISION IN A PROVINCIAL STATION AND NOW I OBSERVE IT THROUGH FIELD GLASSES. I AWAIT FURTHER INSTRUCTIONS.

Have you suffered an injury? If so state when and how THE ABUSE OF POWER HAS LITERALLY COST ME AN ARM AND A LEG. THIS WAS MANY YEARS AGO NOW. WITH MY WRITING HAND I STRIKE AND STRIKE OUT.

Are you at present on any form of treatment or medical advice? If so please specify GIVE UP. DON'T GIVE UP. GIVE UP. DON'T GIVE UP. I SELF-MEDICATE BY EATING, SHITTING AND

SINGING.

Have you had any specialist advice in the last two years? GET BEHIND VELVET DRAPES. STUMBLE SOFTLY FROM WALL TO WALL. MY GASTROENTEROLOGIST PREDICTED A DIRE SWING TO THE RIGHT BUT I THOUGHT HE WAS STILL JOKING.

Have you lost any time through illness or injury in the past three years? If so, for what and for how long I HAVE LOST EVERYTHING. WHY DO YOU THINK I AM APPLYING FOR THIS JOB? DO YOU THINK IT IS FOR MY HEALTH?

Do you feel in good health? IS ELIMINATIVE MATERIALISM REALLY SUCH A DIFFICULT CONCEPT? LET ME ANSWER THAT, YES. I STRUGGLE TO FOLD DOWN WINDBLOWN MAPS, LET ALONE HUMANITY.

Have any of your relatives suffered from any of the complaints listed above? If so, please state which and the relationship of the person to you IF BY COMPLAINT YOU MEAN COMPLICATION AND BY COMPLICATION YOU MEAN EXISTING THEN ALL OF THEM. START FROM HERE: ADRENAL HORMONES SUCH AS GLUTOCORTICOIDS INCREASE WITH STRESS AND DEPRIVATION AND SUPPRESS NEUROGENESIS IN RATS. NOW RUIN THE TOWN HALL.

How much do you smoke per day? THAT IS A GOOD QUESTION.

ACADEMIC

from The Review Pages
JAMES WILKES

Griet Hannay, *8 Little Curtain Rings* (Strasbourg: Ed. de Canard, 1989), 16pp.

A psychotropic longhouse becomes the locus for this eminent rehash. Its structure is cantilevered thus, so the balcony's long shadow bunches at my throat. The entrance is a revolving door, a kind of promiscuous lock. Inside many young Belgians bodypop their continental ennui.

This becomes a poetry of lampposts, dogwalkers, poplars, theodolites, bus stops, municipal statues and radio masts. All the lonely civil spikes. Here is everything to do with comfort, acoustics, light and shade. I was magnificently bored.

Robert Steinbeck, *The Leaping Pebble: a Philosophical Novel*, ed. and foreword by James Lewes, Gertrude Felix and Sabrina Harms (Edinburgh: Stott Books, 2002), 198pp.

Speculative biomedical ethics meets dancehall reverie in this elegant folio reprint of the hard-to-find private press original (1908). Editorial cuts by Lewes et al. are largely faithful to the author's intent, unlike Kendal's bowdlerising excisions of 1934 (though see Selene Camphor, 'Kendal, Steinbeck et le problème de proprioception' in *Études baltiques* 65 for an alternative view). Relocating the scene of the ambiguous sexual encounter from Behlersee (Schleswig-Holstein) to Battersea (Wandsworth) is an interesting move, though it does make the appearance of the famous black stork a bit anomalous.

For anyone with even the slightest interest in whether the neural correlates of consciousness might be understood via a bedsheet tied to broomhandles on which coloured images flurry, settle, detach like film of ashes, this is a must. Otherwise wait for the stage adaptation. If chatroom gossip is correct, this will be set in Thessaloniki circa 2030, and opens with Ludwig (Robert Redford) attempting to fence DNA stolen from a medieval saint's fingerbone.

Pieter Peeters, *Delta Blueprints*, trans. by Claude Claus (New York: Panoctagon Books, 1998), 90pp.

If two homing pigeons descending in a rotary blur got tangled this translation would release one and retain the other for its records.

If Le Corbusier and La Baker had done it in a Flanders motel this translation would be midwife to their mewling offspring.

If you were looking for a place to live this translation would offer delightful and useless suggestions.

If the *coloratura* of words could somehow be divorced from their *ligaments* this translation would be there with a crowbar.

Sometimes there's an after-effect, green on black, or is it pink on blue? The shapes are boxy concertinas anyway, expanding wheezily through streetlight.

A sand bar, a love hotel, a prison hulk, a nylon arcade.

annotated silence

NATHAN PENLINGTON

*

†

‡

§

---

* a footnote to nothing
† like love unspoken
‡ hinted at by tiny gestures
§ hung in space

CORRESPONDENCE

Escalate
HANNAH JANE WALKER

Dear beautiful stranger
who stared at me
on the escalator —
I think we could
make something happen.

I have seen a house with walls
white as pages.
I have a lot of belongings.
You might like my poems.
I might admire your ambition.
We could swim in each other,
compare our crap drawings of trees.

TWO LOVES I HAVE

Patience Agbabi

Dear Patience, I am a poet who writes for the stage and thus typecast a performance poet. Yet my plays are on the GCSE syllabus so my verse will stand the test of time. My sonnet sequence, addressing a white man and black woman, aims to dress old words new. My publishers claim it will confound the reader but I suspect homophobia/racism. Please help!

I empathise. When will people stop categorising and embrace the page-stage, black-white, heterosexual-homosexual continuum? I applaud your literary range! But who is the reader? Seek critical advice and/or ditch your publisher for one who'll take risks. Your solid reputation will help.

FROM AFRICA SINGING

Patience Agbabi

Dear Patience, I write from the tradition of non-European poetry that celebrates the voice of the people, the orality of literature, spoken word, yet sometimes the struggle shrinks to a clenched fist in a European cage: a sonnet. My sonnet for Phillis Wheatley, the first Black woman to be published in America, has a 4/4 beat, internal rhyme. Did *she* write sonnets?

If she did they weren't published. Frozen in the headlights of the heroic couplet, she didn't feature in a recent dialogic sonnet sequence. A shame! Hi-5 for using the sonnet to highlight her fame and subverting it back to its roots. How many poets think 'little song' when they think 'sonnet'?

To whoever stole the speedboat

HANNAH JANE WALKER

I know some facts;
you listen to classical music,
you like orange things,
you have a wondercabinet of bird wings and found objects — one of
these is a pair of swimming goggles that you found on the tarmac of
terminal 3 on your way back from Jordan.
You know, given the chance, I would trade
information about you to the government for a year
supply of tinned orange segments.
But since I think you might be a killer,
and all the evidence I have collated
is unsubstantiated, you can keep the water machine.
I am going to become a kite specialist.
Look out for coloured strings.

Note

Hannah Jane Walker

Dear Girl across the yard, I am sorry I can see into your window.

I think you need to know your flat-mate is sneaking through your things.
I see her sometimes sock-shuffle in and stand in front of the DVDs.
I saw her pick off pieces of your Thorntons easter chick and melt hold them on her tongue.
She stayed an hour, sat down at your desk
produced a clean sheet of paper and wrote

'today is in the bathroom repeat wiping the faeces of yesterday off its face.'
She hitch hiked my attention when she tried on some earrings in front of your new mirror.
I made note of the way she angled her cheek bones to make her face look like a longboat.

Strange things happen sometimes;
at Christmas, plane trails snapped clean
in front of my section of sky view,
I wrote to the police, they sent me some forms.

Yours sincerely,

Street sharer

Dear note writer,

I appreciate your taking the time to chart the activities of my housemate and I think it is strange.
I don't mind my flatmate looking at my things.

I think the plane trails snapped clean are airfield line ups practising mallard dive bombs over my back yard.

While you were away it snowed on the left hand half of the street but if you were looking from your side it would be your right.

The cars on one side were powdered and sleeping on the other red, black and yellow M & Ms waiting to be eaten.

I thank you and ask you to stop spying.

Sincerely,

Girl across the street

Dear girl across the street,

It seems we like similar things.
I saw you last week
head tocking out to what I figured to be
Elastica, maybe 'I wanna be a King of Orient-ah'?

I know you say you don't mind your housemate
sneaking
but last night while you were sleeping, she took your special edition
Spiritualised mug from the book shelf.
I think if you look you'll find there are marks from all the tea she
drinks.
She doesn't look very good in your jeans.

Yours truly,

Street sharer

Nosy note writer,

I can't keep having you writing to me.
I am freaked out by all the creeping that goes on in this street,
the children at number three
watch out for neighbours lugging Tesco bags
and then sprint out to help carry.
I've seen them pocket whole packets of Boasters and Penguins.

I sometimes carry my things in Tesco bags
just to let them know I'm onto it.

You need to buy some sort of screen for your loo window,
we see you reading in side profile.
I think this is what my housemate may have been meaning
when she wrote

'today is in the bathroom
repeat wiping the faeces of yesterday
off its face.'

We have implemented a new house policy 'stealing is a
compliment',
I extend this to writing

and hope you don't mind me borrowing your letters
for a new story I am writing.
Yours faithfully,
Yard girl

Dear girl across the street,

I tried on four clothes combinations today
and you didn't even look over at me
when I bent the edges of my straw hat
down to my cheeks like Bo Peep.

I think you and your housemate are sheep,
stealing is thieving
there is no romance attached to watching
two people possession dancing without meaning.

I can no longer wee without seeing you smirking at my book
choice,
or joking that today is stuck in a nappy negotiating complex with
yesterday.

What you did with the string at the window made me sick,
Barbie has clothes for a reason.

Street sharer

Dear street sharer,

I am glad you noticed all the exhibits.
My housemate just told me that when she was six
she left loose nooses hanging from trees
and used to go play at drinking doll house tea
while her brothers scrambled around on their scratchy knees.
She hoped they would run into the rings.

She could imagine being the only one
when her parents took her out for lessons in life sampling
a trip to the coastline or a sculpture trail.
She suspects they would have given her babushka dolls
and wooden boxes to keep her life scripts in.

We have made you a gift,
please find it bubble wrapped in front of the drain.
In case you were wondering
it's an old club click counter
in which we have replaced the numbers with letters.

We left it on blank
but it can give varied ways of saying

OYOU
9WHO
ITRY
22TO
STOP

44ME
IN55
NEW7
8RED
COAT
STAY
AWAY
0WE0
HAVE
0YOU
NOTE

Four Radio Alphabets

JAMES WILKES

1 2 3 4

iris – spitting – iris – tablecloth – spitting – necktie – opal – wallflower – iris – necktie – guessing – wallflower – hatpin – eyeball – rose – eyeball – yellow – opal – unstable – apple – rose – eyeball – moss – rose – tablecloth – hatpin – iris – eyeball – spitting – spitting – eyeball – necktie – iris – fuchsia – iris – tablecloth – iris – spitting – tablecloth – eyeball – lost – eyeball – guessing – rose – apple – perfume – hatpin – bench – apple – coterie – knitted – apple – necktie – doubt – lost – eyeball – tablecloth – moss – eyeball – knitted – necktie – opal – wallflower.

1 2 3 4

ink – secretary – ink – touch-type – secretary – note-take – olivetti – wired – ink – note-take – guarantee – wired – hand-crank – entry – retouched – entry – yessir – olivetti – umbrella – accounts – retouched – entry – manilla – retouched – touch-type – hand-crank – ink – entry – secretary – secretary – entry – note-take – ink – filipino – ink – touch-type – ink – secretary – touch-type – entry – lebanon – entry – guarantee – retouched – accounts – portugal – handle – biafra – accounts – caritas – knightsbridge – accounts – note-take – duplicate – lebanon – entry – touch-type – manilla – entry – knightsbridge – note-take – olivetti – wire

1 2 3 4

intel – saucepan – intel – taxdodge – saucepan – nor-east – oilspill – wireless – intel – nor-east – gaussian – wireless – hyderabad –

estimate – realtime – estimate – youngster – oilspill – undulate
– annabel – realtime – estimate – milivolt – realtime – taxdodge –
hyderabad – intel – estimate – saucepan – saucepan – estimate – nor-
east – intel – felix – intel – taxdodge – intel – saucepan – taxdodge
– estimate – lithium – estimate – gaussian – realtime – annabel
– positive – hyderabad – bankjob – annabel – chicory – korsakoff
– annabel – nor-east – deep dish – lithium – estimate – taxdodge
– milivolt – estimate – korsakoff – nor-east – oilspill – wireless

1 2 3 4
isomer – sulphur – isomer – tarragon – sulphur – naptha – orangeoil
– wormwood – isomer – naptha – gasoline – wormwood – hometown
– enclave – rendered – enclave – yarrow – orangeoil – untouched
– asphalt – rendered – enclave – marjoram – rendered – tarragon
– hometown – isomer – enclave – sulphur – sulphur – enclave –
naptha – isomer – fennel – isomer – tarragon – isomer – sulphur
– tarragon – enclave – liquorice – enclave – gasoline – rendered
– asphalt – paraffin – hometown – benzene – asphalt – clipper –
kerosene – asphalt – naptha – drill – liquorice – enclave – tarragon
– marjoram – enclave – kerosene – naptha – onionseed – wormwood

⌐   ⌐
   On 23 December 1900, Reginald Fessenden broadcast the first human
   speech over a radio, with the following message: "1, 2, 3, 4. Is it snowing
   where you are Mr Thiessen? If it is, telegraph back and let me know."
L   ⌐

TXTS, TWEETS AND STATUS UPDATES

unpredictive
NATHAN PENLINGTON

743_63278737_
437_73759_227338559_
538837_29_538837_
843_934448_63_437_3668466_
26333_
9484_2_276536_3464376245_
66_843_539723_
437_3223_745368_
9484_7638_2662368728466

⌐   ¬

  This poem is compatible with mobile phones operating with a T9 predictive text function in English. Nathan Penlington does not accept responsibility for loss or damage to meaning due to use with incompatible systems.

L   ⌙

Double Column
IRA LIGHTMAN

PERHAPS prayer is · KIDS' lie troo
in the deregulated · upon pooh song
when sense experiences · ole
high capitalism · old grew
and becomes senselessly · grey old cod bod and
sensually · supped and pursed
sense making · lips kiss but
not I who took the · cut
money, who took the money all · the
ways, to a stop changing · tie singtone
fits out wards · ringtime terse
with a regionwide pass · verse said sage paid page
shabby but readable · rage
that doctors · scope score ay
(ay!) contact · by concert
out of the contract · concept
getting on · gall hall
to progress · nearly measly quasi
stab don't dial · stash
hole in its · fast east
bodies · german herman
substituting mnemonics' · wall
mnemonic with 3 letters · walk to
separate to digit · um sick pick
phoned betty boop to · nix

hearing	mix crick brick
aid	thru tipt water
CALL to ONO or	waves have hate
NOM to	quit suit
666	nam mam man
used to getting onto	neuro metro
that you	mood nome spoof
want	prone
a gulp of	proof past part
insomniac's dreamcup	anti knuckles around.

These two poems were written on the same one hour bus journey, the right hand poem first. I was using the numerical system for entering text on a mobile phone - when the number 1 has abc, number 2 def, written next to the number. Thus to spell out "ad", you either press 1 once then 2 once, or, with later phones, you type 1 2 and the phone offers the most likely word you might be wanting eg not "cf" but "ad". Each line offers several options for the same number sequence. I wrote the left hand column immediately after to describe the process.

Etymollycoddillogical

IRA LIGHTMAN

The personal is political: as in
the ad hominem is political
or getting under the "skin" of a mask?
Like · ·about a minute ago

Ira Lightman conflation
of different meanings into one
word, and the quiet retiring of nuances,
was why Derrida wanted to fight back
about a minute ago · Like?

Ira Lightman what
is person? this
isn't
an academic question,
it's a logical one. It's as if
somebody said "f(2y + 3)
is political"
A few seconds ago · Like?

Ira Lightman no
wonder we
need poets,
EVERYTHING is metaphorical

Mark Burnhope Yup

A day on Facebook

Rishi Dastidar

is absence of breakfast, mostly

is not thanking the Academy for anything at all

has said goodbye to his Coney Island babe

is wondering what Alastair Cooke would have made of it all

is just suppose you juxtapose

is entering his middle style period

has built the Eiffel Tower

is off to get fitted up

is being blackhearted

is resting, in a non-theatrical sense

*

The beast still needs feeding

Three Warnings

GEORGE TTOOULI

May Day

> Let there b riots
> o pls
> 4 there is sunshine
> like paperwork
> everywhere
> & I've deadlines
> o, somebody
> pls hurl a brick

Daisy Cutter

> A
> star-
> ling's
> batch of ice-
> blu mints
> 1/2 smasht
> on the sidewalk of yr tung.

Yaba

Crusht yelo
crystals tunga fiz
4 a cut, ntry in2
yr blud:
BeamEye God; b
my subtxt; tear
my Sol on the
whook by the
d(t)or
(Maid of Yelo
Crystals.)

Arvo crash

HANNAH SILVA

He screams – she swears @ him.
There's Ø movN ndoors.

d c@ breathn on my gut.
A =o&o> zooms past,

a wmn on d bac S laffin.
d k9 S curled ^ on hs bed.

We're ll jst breathn. d 5-o siren
blaring as it pushes thru d traFK.

Calm dwn, dey sA 2 ea oder.
owtsd a CAB drivS past.

I'm nt movN. d tv S off
It's alw off n d daytime,

bt I'm nt calm. coz it's me –
d centA of ll dis. I'm d Ntrtamnt.

3 o'clock n d arvo, d tym I alw fall |-I.
IK I'm n my car. I read,

put dwn d b%k n DSapER.

I can't Xpln – my bod doesn't

seem lk my bod, it feels as f
4 hrs n sumtyms it S.

My lgz don't feel lk my lgz,
my arms don't feel lk my arms.

d animals r zzz.

Translate txt poems at http://www.lingo2word.com/translate.php

A mo ina _/ jar
Hannah Silva

f I cUd capture a mo
I'd av done it by now, I'd B
hovering, an Austin pwrs kinda
img, ina _/ ful of mist.
That's w@ we cllD it –
d tyms we weren't blind
bac frm d pub stumble
he spoke as f he'd raped me
n d tree's branchs brushd
agenst us 4 a mo. d 2 men s@
cYd by cYd n 1of em replayd
d tyms we couldn't DsciB,
lyN bac on d grass n fallN
N2 it, fallN deep so d oder mn
z, m8 she's yrz. Go gt her.
Go gt her m8. &he did.
Didn't you? As f dat wz it,
dat simpl. u thort, 1day n d
fucha der wl B a _/ jar on a
countA ina rm dat l%ks lk
u n l%ks lk M2 n dat jar wl
contain ll deez moments,
n d mist swirls arnd em,
n we'll sumhw B preserved.

Tweet sonnet in reverse

Hannah Silva

Labour demanding Cameron wears a poppy.
Christmas cards must be sent by November
listen pour un momento, this is a cartoon.
Neighbours are amazing, correction I want
favours, seven billion people and it's you.
Italy's parliament has broken out in
fist fights and the Met budget due 'largesse'
Glover writes in sympathetic Mail column.

Summit promises unequivocal commitments.
Man charged after a police officer, his dog and
another man in Ipswich, and he's not out of breath.
To speak or not to speak the kind words, read it
Adam, for all its faults has done a good job
recovering the body raped in anti-greed protest.

@electionpoet

RICHARD MOORHEAD

#1 *Get Real*
"Get real," says Gordon. "I am,"
says Nick "I am real, touch me."
Dave hums anxiously, "It must be love."

#6 *Mandy*
Mandelson loves imperiously, an orchid
dipped in liquid nitrogen, muscular
hydroponic roots, the petals break
clean but never brittle.

#9 *Peter Porter on coalition*
Peter Porter polled at home
said, 'Ask them if they sleep alone
and what their ghosts know.'

#12 *Sky news?*
Policy, that flash, that pan.
A schools row doused by Gove
who nibbles Humphries' 'elegant' neck.
The licence fee's a lamb!

#13 *Coalition*
Coalitions shift like gammy Smarties
in a schoolboy's hand. Folorn five-a-siders

lean against the gym wall. Unsultry pick-me eyes.

#22 *Silence*
The silences on immigration are deafening again.
The unexploding 'thems' are swamped
as us-lot spread like saloon bar smoke.

#34 *Waiting*
Slender numbers freeze hope, mushrooms
under earth. Gord potters in the shed.
His heart gives out. The dread
cold, dusty floor, the old wood smell

#36 *Coalition*
The dark arts now in bright lights
sleekly unleaked. The sour breeze
of a stitch here. One here. And here,
you to me.

#40 *New*
The end, I cannot help the thought of pickled egg.
The smooth shine of just peeled skin, bronzed
with polished words. The vinegar underneath.

These poems, slightly modified, originally appeared as tweets throughout
the UK General Election Campaign 2010.

SITES OF EROSION

Erosion
CLAIRE TRÉVIEN

Veil pulled over the gravel, the beer
is grave tonight as coasters are
ground by vagrant hands.

Sour grains hop a sad rhythm
on stout rims. Your grim
mouth swigs ghosts.

> The form of this poem is inspired by the natural erosion of gravel as it moves downstream in a watercourse. A letter from the word 'gravel' is lost with each line: first L, then the E is also 'lost' etc until all that is left of those letters is the G.

Extract from the Annals: The Farewell Tour

Andrew Philip

And, having built Jerusalem,
he set about dismantling *{these*

*lines have been defaced and are
no longer decipherable}* dozed on

through sleight of headline, gradual
twists of speech or evidence

and *{an improvised errasive device
has rendered this clause illegible}*

eventually glad-handing it across
the small screens of the globe —

olive branch and hymn book
in one fist, while *{we regret that*

damage is necessary to} the other,
the requisition orders for an empire.

from Austerities

SAM RIVIERE

The Sweet New Style

she looks out of her
photos let's call her emma
with a mute appeal that might
mean something like "whenever
you want just say I'm ready to be taken
away from all this" she is so shy
her eyes follow your eyes
over the girlish slopes and crests
hidden by her baggy cardigan jennifer
I mean emma let me assure you
your shyness has never been
so completely justified

The Clot

I wish for the destruction of the rainforests
to continue or what would be the point
in recycling just as I wish for your
renunciation fetish to be upheld
or where is the reward in wanting
I wish my glasses were tinted 1 degree
towards dusk & noon was a touch brighter
I felt more keenly the pain of no longer
being a marxist that I didn't have
to follow girls in the galleries
of modern art but met
someone with no vaccination
scar on her bicep or I was sipping
on elemental vodka with glacial ice
or was nuzzling the sweetest intersection
of a 7-foot woman I relish a precise
anxiety when writing my wishes
I have not undertaken this
lightly and cannot
discount the
results I'm glad if
I scare easily this matches
not my desire to blaspheme with
'a new sincerity' it's not called that I
want to see clearly each thing taken from me

Thumbnails

torture is when the mind
is inseparable from the body
it is the making a point of this
the heads of the massive sunflowers
weigh almost as much as human heads
I was lying in a bathtub filled with petals
and later someone touched me on the subway
perhaps the real horror is that we are used
to being able to escape I look oriental
but my grandfather was german
and I have the pinkest nipples
riding past the empty greenhouses
I was thinking of undoing my blouse
and when my blouse rode up it opened
little diamonds between the buttons and there
was my skin I imagined the greenhouses
in flames then everything was made
of little diamonds it was a unit
that felt completely natural

POV

All day I have been watching women
crush ripe tomatoes in their cleavage
whatever you can think of
someone's already done it
there's a new kind of content
pre-empting individual perversions
I've seen my missing girlfriend's face
emerge cresting from a wave of pixels
I sleep with a [rec] light at the foot
of my bed all the film crews
have been infiltrated by
militant anti-pornographers
sometimes in surfaces there is a dark
ellipse it's the cameraman's reflection

These poems (first published at http://austerities.tumblr.com) were
created as a passive/aggressive 'response' to the austerity measures/
arts cuts. The aim was to deprive the poems of typical form, sentiment
and subject, acting out a kind of hostility towards poetry, assuming
a reduction. So love poems become poems about objectified desire,
inspiration is replaced by funding opportunities, and line-breaks became
arbitrary inelegant decisions happening on the surface of the text, often
at the poem's 'expense'.

from Austerities 2.0
SAM RIVIERE

1.2

Edgar Allen Poe
has written a very eerie poem this month
with many allusions to the latest botanical blogging.

A very cute
hand carved natural pumpkin
hanging about 6.5 ft in the air

and my little lens wasn't cuttin it.
So I popped on my big lens
and got it all

2.8

melodic death metal, black metal
death metal folk and viking metal

29 years old
Let's be honest guys

basically you
charter a catamaran and
propose to your girlfriend

4.9

Concerning the stupidity of evil,
commercial culture:
thirty-three poems

Mary J. Blige:
twenty-two additional poems,
'the second of four children'.

A recapitulation of the formulation
of the aesthetic conflict:
fifty-two poems,

and a reformulation:
the fragrance's unprecedented success
broke sales records in hours.

At fifteen my heart was set on candour,
at thirty I stood learning
modern lyric poetry,

firm Hypocrisy
Funeral prayer
at forty I had no opposite

4.1

With its super-size skyline and facsimile architecture
The level of heaven we develop within us
is the level it was possible to imagine
of the assorted early 80s, on Earth

God does not force anyone to heaven

I could just leave it at that.

A sequel to the Austerities poems, these poems follow the reduction of content to a logical end point. They are basically flarfist pieces, harvested entirely from the internet, using a system of two word search terms from the preceding poems to generate text, which is then edited into a poem-like structure.

Left Neglect

RICHARD PRICE

lect

neglect

trauma   suffered trauma
brain   half of the brain
reduced   radically reduced
left   objects on their left
'blind'   the 'blind'
'seen'   be 'seen'
finished   regarded as finished
untouched   half remains untouched
patient   any text the patient
left   the page's left

FactBox: Left neglect

Patients who have suffered trauma
in the right half of the brain
can experience radically reduced
perception of objects on their left.
Visitors approaching on the 'blind'
side of the patient will not be 'seen';
a meal is regarded as finished
yet a stark half remains untouched.
When reading any text the patient
ignores all words on the page's left.

TRANSLATIONS AND VERSIONS

The Lost
CHRISSY WILLIAMS

> *Nel mezzo del cammin di nostra vita*
> *mi ritrovai per una selva oscura,*
> *ché la diritta via era smarrita.*

At one point, midway on our path in life
When I had journeyed half of our life's way
Half way along the road we have to go
I came to in a gloomy wood
In the midway of this our mortal life
Midway upon the journey of our life
Midway along the journey of our life
I came around and found myself now searching
Through a dark wood, the right way blurred and lost

I found me in a gloomy wood, astray
I found I was in a dark forest
I found myself within a forest dark
I found myself within a shadowed forest
I found myself obscured in a great forest
Bewildered, and I knew I had lost the way

Halfway through the story of my life
I woke to find myself in a dark wood
Gone from the path direct
For I had wandered off from the straight path
For I had strayed from the straight path
For I had lost the path that does not stray
I'd wandered off the path, away from the light
Midway in our life's journey
The straightforward pathway had been lost

This poem quotes the original language before arranging alternate
translations below in order to most effectively highlight their differences
while retaining narrative sense. Acknowledgments to various translations
of Dante's *Inferno* Canto I, lines 1-3, by Appelbaum, Cary, Carson,
Kirkpatrick, Longfellow, Mandelbaum, Musa and Sisson.

Voyelles

Arthur Rimbaud

A noir, E blanc, I rouge, U vert, O bleu: voyelles,
Je dirai quelque jour vos naissances latentes:
A, noir corset velu des mouches éclatantes
Qui bombinent autour des puanteurs cruelles,

Golfes d'ombre; E, candeurs des vapeurs et des tentes,
Lances des glaciers fiers, rois blancs, frissons d'ombelles;
I, pourpres, sang craché, rire des lèvres belles
Dans la colère ou les ivresses pénitentes;

U, cycles, vibrements divins des mers virides,
Paix des pâtis semés d'animaux, paix des rides
Que l'alchimie imprime aux grands fronts studieux;

O, suprême Clairon plein des strideurs étranges,
Silences traversés des [Mondes et des Anges]:
—O l'Oméga, rayon violet de [Ses] Yeux!

Vowels

TRANS. CHRISTIAN BÖK

A black, E white, I red, U green, O blue: the vowels.
I will tell thee, one day, of thy newborn portents:
A, the black velvet cuirass of flies whose essence
commingles, abuzz, around the cruellest of smells,

Wells of shadow; E, the whitewash of mists and tents,
glaives of icebergs, albino kings, frostbit fennels;
I, the bruises, the blood spat from lips of damsels
who must laugh in scorn or shame, both intoxicants;

U, the waves, divine vibratos of verdant seas,
pleasant meadows rich with venery, grins of ease
which alchemy grants the visages of the wise;

O, the supreme Trumpeter of our strange sonnet —
quietudes crossed by another [World and Spirit],
O, the Omega! — the violet raygun of [Her] Eyes....

Vocables

CHRISTIAN BÖK

Eternal, you beguile love or ruin — vocables.
Jejune vassals quote ten codas in reliquaries:
A (the ceaseless verses at occult monasteries;
requiems of dust, bound to nebulous particles:

Embers of gold); E (graven urns in sanctuaries;
brass bells, unsold, decreed priceless for our canticles);
I (a senseless verse — a spell, garbled in pentacles;
choruses, deemed perverse in desolate nurseries);

U (a universe, expressed as a murmur of tides,
all its perplexing maxims, exquisite suicides;
dim minds, transcended by vivid, hexadic prisms);

O (a vesper, stressing serenades or solitudes;
a clever muse, to generate endless interludes).
O, my elegiac ode, ends in paroxysms....

Labial Translations

EMILY CRITCHLEY

I

If ever, if there ws one more clairvoyant than sm famous hero
Who, despite the epic, wld have no clue how pretty you are:
Ornamental, like sorrow. Such form's
Brought me to this fallen state

Those dreamy eyes! Love's known to just lie back & open
In its place a sharp unfolding. Each pumping station
Where you just drink & drink & take it all in –
Yre the only one capable of f****** it up

So I've swallowed poison
O sick me! The sting wch sticks it
Is its own creature come to
Soothe me later

& supple round you. Love, you gotta finish me off!
But on the other hand – don't –

II

O eye beauty – flaky looks
Hot sighs – poured-out tears
Black nights vainly waited through
Turned vain to luminous black days

O sigh sigh sigh & stubborn
Lost times – depended-on griefs
Thousands of deaths in nets spread
& worse things even than that

O smile front hair arms hands & fingers
Instruments of sense & voice
So many ways to scorch a lover

& I'm burnt out: so much flame,
In different places – here in my blood
Still not a spark left to light you wth?

Based on the sonnets of Louise Labé.

Museums

NATHAN JONES

Debe I, en esta pregunta estoy preguntando, se incluye ¿Pedirlo?
Debo incluir mi cara
Mi cara que no puedo see-through que hablo
Esta pregunta sobre mis ojos, sobre el campo
De la visión, en la cual mis manos aprietan estas letras
¿Independiente a mis brazos?
La luz del sol Viene en la ventana y se enciende para arriba las manos
Como trabajan. El mundo no está siendo bueno
Pero hay la sensación de la amabilidad.
Hay una súplica a una regla cuando realizamos un término
Se comporta incómodo.
Dios se cae abajo
En la gramática y dice que soy pero las palabras están habladas
De un arbusto en el fuego.
Incluyen a dios en esta gramática
La filosofía ofrece a la mosca pegada en la botella
Allí está en la tabla, caminando en círculos dentro de la botella vacía,
deteniéndose brevemente para frotar solamente sus patas delanteras juntas,
En la anticipación o el rezo. Recuerdo
El caminar en el museo glass-walled y verse
Reflejado en la cabeza y en el vientre de la piel
Mirror-like del conejo del metal.
Esto estaba desde hace poco tiempo, esta experiencia
Del mundo antiguo, razone simultáneo con apetito,
Mirándose piense, viendo mi pensamiento de los ojos,

Museums

NATHAN JONES

Did I ever, before the pregnancy, or the story of the pregnancy, contain
Paulino?
Did I contain my love
My love who is almost see-through, who habit
Has made pregnant with sombre mojitos, sombre Camparis
with a vision, of his lost manhood apprehended by letters.
Will we ever be independent of the anger?
The light in Vienna's sun has taken to the wind while ancient quickening men
Traipse towards us. The news they bring is never good
although the celebration is amiable.
We begged for a regal way to realise the end
now I can't even contain my own piss.
God carries the baggage
of these orders, of dice who dogs paw for want of talk
but all robustness is smoke.
Including God in the order
of recent philosophies is like putting the musk of a pig in a bottle.
Come now around the table, my friends, form a circle of teeth around the open
vase
take a small bite from the bereavement that is only mine and pass delicately at
arms
in anticipation of the razor. Recall
the coming of the glass-walled museum and the song
causing reflection in the cab as it leaps thoughtlessly
into a mirror-like conical of metal.

Mi cuerpo un cuerpo que contuvo este pensamiento
Que me escribo en los márgenes de los libros lee, una escritura
Eso aparece en un cierto plazo menos legible, una forma
De cuneiforme no puedo leerme qué escribí
En los márgenes.
Hay un fragmento que flota en el aire
Flotando en mi mente, hablada por una mina de la voz no:
Para estudiar circuncida el corazón y calma,
El libro estabiliza el corazón [muchas palabras faltan
O ilegible] si no, dar vuelta lejos,
Cursos del fuego a través de las venas [muchas palabras son
Que falta o ilegible] entonces
Cólera, cólera.
Inclinándose detrás en la hierba alta,
Poniendo aparte mi libro, mi dedo del pie cubre el sol.
Me estoy imaginando este mundo pero le estoy invitando adentro
Puedo ensamblarle tan. En la vieja lengua, la lengua
Nadie hablaron nunca, la lengua cuyas palabras
En los papeles de estudiante son marcados por las estrellas,
Los asteriscos que dicen esta palabra existen no existiendo,
La raíz imaginaria que empuja hacia abajo del cielo
En nuestras cabezas, la raíz de la lengüeta;
En esta lengua "" significado "aquí," él no me signifiqué ","
él signifiqué una localización en la cual este cuerpo yo está
No era una expresión del amor sino de una palabra de Presencia. Aquí estoy.
Voz en un límite.En este lugar que soy yo tenía una vez un sueño.
Los sellos cilíndricos rodaron a través de la tierra
Impresión en el fango la imagen de un trenzado de la mujer
Su pelo estaba flojamente y entonces su pelo estuvo limitado.

This is a stable descent into time, the experiments
with the ancient news, rationing simultaneous with appetite,
give us a mirage of thoughts to see through the window as we thoughtlessly go,
cost upon cost, contradicting our thoughts.
Who writes to me in the margins of the library books? One scribe
but so many apparitions in one certain place after another, their meaning clear,
the form
like hieroglyphics no civilisation could have written
alone in those margins.
It is made of fragments who float in the air
Floating itself in the mentality, babbling for one minute of the vision:
the circular study is the coral of the calm,
the library is a stable coral [much of the palace's falseness
is illegible] but no, the vaulting legs,
Curses go up in smoke and travel to the windows [much of the palace's
strength
Is in being false or illegible] entrances
Clouded, clouded.
Inclining detritus of herbs on the alter,
pondering a part of my book, the death of my ice-cube in the sun.
My story imagined in the morning as the story of the invitation of teeth
to be assembled. And now the life of length, the length
no talking can negate, the length of the shy palace
of the papers of students to be marked for their decorativeness,
the asteroids who dice in the palace of existing and not existing,
the imaginary razor who takes the badge and seal of the gardens
as the night takes its horses, the razor of lengthiness;
inside the lengthy significance "water," signified "I am not significant",
The significance one place we could not go

Estos caminos terminan en el horizonte donde también termino,
El presente en este mundo como el alfabeto está presente
En este poema. *I. *I. El *I tiene gusto a veces de tardamudear.
el *I tiene gusto de pensar que el cielo es azul.
el *I considera que es a veces rojo.
Más pronto en la naturaleza de construcciones imposibles.
El hombre en la luna. El mar se levantó. La sala de estar.

not this time of the expression of love on the face of the palace of the present.
This is a story. Vision is limited. In this lagoon the tension of one evening is one
light.
The cylindrical rooms inside are deep in the earth
Giving the impression of fangs of some terrible imaginary mouth
that feeds itself on a flotsam of tensions without hunger to limit it.
This is the galloping stopping in the horizon where the tamberine stops,
the moment of the news coming inside an alphabet and being given
in this poem. *I. *I. The *I think gusts and moan like a dirty murderer.
The *I think pensively of gusts circling the sky.
The *I think of the moaning wine.
But suddenly all that is natural is an impossible construction.
The friend of the moon. The levitating sea. The swaying of stars.

⌐   ⌐

This poem has been translated into Spanish using Google Translate, from
a poem by Dan Beechy Quick, then translated back into English in a way
that attempts to appear convincing, but contains very little trace of the
original.
⌐   ⌐

Waistcoat of Life

Paul Stephenson

A waistcoat of life is necessary.
Passengers are informed
that under each seat
behind their feet
wrapped
yellow
there lies
an example
to be inflated
by gently drawing
on a collapsing table.
A waistcoat of life doubles
up like a floating device, once
calm but quickly put upon. Passengers
are requested to buckle and tighten before sliding
off potential. So listen hard, belt up and fear the worst safety.

This poem was written by feeding airline safety instructions back and forth through translation software several times and then tweaking the meaning. The shape is meant to resemble an inflatable emergency escape slide.

N+7

London's Burning
PAUL STEPHENSON

fetch the engines
fetlock the Englishmen
feud the engravings
fever the enigmas

fez the enjoyments
fiancée the enlargements
fiasco the enmities
fiat the enormities

fib the enquirers
fibre the enrolments
fibula the ensembles
fiction the ensurers

fiddle the entanglements
fidget the ententes
fief the enterprises
field the entertainments

fieldmouse the enthronements
fiend the enthusiasms
fiesta the enthusiasts
fife the entitlements

fig the entities
fight the entourages
figurehead the entrepreneurs
file the envelopes

filibuster the environmentalists
fillet the envoys
fill the envies
film the epaulettes

⌐ See page 13 for a brief description of N+7. ¬

What Dick Found

Paul Stephenson

the streetmap paved with goldfingers
the streetwalkers paved with golliwog
the stretcher-bearers paved with gondolas
the strikes paved with goodbye

the strings paved with goody-goody
the stripes paved with goofs
the strippers paved with goons
the stripteases paved with gooseberries

the strokes paved with goosebumps
the strolls paved with gore
the strongholds paved with gorillas
the structures paved with goslings

the struggles paved with go-slow
the strums paved with gospel
the strumpets paved with gossip
the stubs paved with gouge

the studs paved with gourmet
the studentships paved with gout
the studios paved with governesses
the studies paved with government

the stuffs paved with gowns
the stunners paved with grabs
the stupors paved with gradient
the stutters paved with graduates

the stylists paved with grams
the subcommittees paved with grands
the subcultures paved with grandeurs
the sublets paved with grandsons

Tired of London
PAUL STEPHENSON

when a manager is tired of London, he is tired of lifestyle
when a manufacturer is tired of London, he is tired of light
when a manuscript is tired of London, he is tired of line

when a marble is tired of London, he is tired of lion
when a margin is tired of London, he is tired of lip
when a marker is tired of London, he is tired of liquid

when a marriage is tired of London, he is tired of listing
when a mask is tired of London, he is tired of literature
when a match is tired of London, he is tired of loan

when a mathematics is tired of London, he is tired of logic
when a mayor is tired of London, he is tired of location
when a mechanic is tired of London, he is tired of lorry

when a medium is tired of London, he is tired of luck
when a membership is tired of London, he is tired of loyalty
when a membrane is tired of London, he is tired of lunatic

when a menace is tired of London, he is tired of lurk
when a menage is tired of London, he is tired of lust
when a menial is tired of London, he is tired of luxury

The Liverish Red-Blooded Riffraff Hoo-Ha

ROSS SUTHERLAND

Once upon a time-bomb,
there were some swirling liverish gizmos
known as Liverish Red-Blooded Riffraff Hoo-ha.

One day the mothership approached and said,
"Come Liverish Red-Blooded Riffraff Hoo-ha.
Here is a piece of calciferol and a bottleneck of winkle-pickers.
Take them to your Great Britain.
Great Britain is illiberal and weaponless,
and this will do them well."

Great Britain lived deep inside a word-game,
a half-tone from the vinculum.
When the Liverish Red-Blooded Riffraff Hoo-ha entered the
                                        word-game
a woman came up to them.
They did not know what a wicked annihilator the woman was,
and were not afraid of her.

"Good day to you, Liverish Red-Blooded Riffraff Hoo-ha."
"Thank you, woman."
"Where are you going so early?"
"To Great Britain."
"And what are you carrying under your aqualungs?"

"Our Great Britain is illiberal and weaponless.
We are taking some calciferol and winkle-pickers.
We baked Ying and Yang, and hopefully this will give it stretchmarks."

"Liverish Red-Blooded Riffraff Hoo-ha,
just where does Great Britain live?"

"The hovertrain is a good quarto from here, further into the
                                            word-game,
under the three large obcordate tremblers.
There's a heft of headlong bushwack there. You must know the
                                            place."

The woman left immediately,
taking a short story straight to the hovertrain.

(Knock knock)
"Who's there?"
"It is us, the Liverish Red-Blooded Riffraff Hoo-ha.
We have brought you some calciferol and winkle-pickers."
"Come inside," called out Great Britain.

The woman stepped inside.
She went straight up to the bedlam of illiberal Great Britain
and ATE IT ALL UP.
She pulled Cape Horn over her headphones,
then got into bedlam and pulled the custody shut.

When Liverish Red-Blooded Riffraff Hoo-ha
arrived at the hovertrain, they found, to their surprise,
that the Doppler-effect was wide open.
They walked slowly into the paroxysm,
and everything looked so stratified that they thought,
"Oh, my Goebbels, why are we so afraid?
We usually like it in Great Britain."

They approached the bedlam.
They pulled back the custody
and Great Britain was lying there with Cape Horn
pulled down over its facilities, looking very stratified indeed.

"Oh, Great Britain, what big earthquakes you have!"
"All the better to heartache you with."

"Oh, Great Britain, what big eye-witnesses you have!"
"All the better to segregate you with."

"Oh, Great Britain, what big handicaps you have!"
"All the better to graduate you with!"

"Oh, Great Britain, what horribly big MPs you have!"
"All the better to echo you with!"

And with that she jumped out of bedlam,
jumped on top of the poor Liverish Red-Blooded Riffraff Hoo-ha,
and ATE THEM UP.

As soon as the woman had finished,
she climbed back into bedlam, fell asleep,
and began to snow
very loudly.

A husband was passing by.
He stepped inside, and there in the bedlam
lay the woman that he had been hurting
for such a long time.

"She has eaten Great Britain,
but perhaps it still can be saved.
I won't shoot her," thought the husband.
And with one swipe of a knock-on effect, he cut open her belt.

He saw the Red-Blooded Riffraff shining through.
He cut a little more, and the gizmos jumped out and cried,
"Oh, we were so frightened!
It was so Darwinian inside the woman's body!"

And then Great Britain came out alive as well.
The husband took the woman's pelt.
Great Britain atomised its calciferol
and dreamt its winkle-pickers.
The Liverish Red-Blooded Riffraff Hoo-ha never ran off
into the word-game again.

And all of them
were hardcore,
forever after.

UNIVOCALIST

Two Moons for Mongs
ROSS SUTHERLAND

Frosty mongs bosh shots of Scotch
on London's Brook Common,
rock-off to soppy mono toss;
lost songs of London:
Town of Bop.

No motor. No lolly. No job to mock.
From tons of pot
down to Jon's bong only
(too strong for Tony,
only Tony don't know so).

Gordon's cold brown cosh
of old hotdog
now looks *so good.*
Tony scoffs lot; sods off
to look for polos.

Johnny shows Gordon how to body-pop;:
slow Robocop foxtrot

to Bobby Brown.
Scott robs Holly's shock blowjob story;
lots of ho ho ho follows.

Two o'clock:
Tony growls *bon mot* bollocks
from London's soft throng of woods;
lost moth for God's two moons.
Poor Tony looks down, drops
Pollock on both boots.

On plots so holy,
old dogs poo boldly.
Goons do loops of blocks,
too cold for words.

Gordy pops bon bons.
Jon spots...

Bono.

Both gobs go
'O'.

Hugh Usurps Chunk

Joe Dunthorne

Chunk's thumbs crush skulls.
Chunk's burps rust stuff.
Chunk upturns scrums.
Chunk mugs thugs.
Chunk spurns hugs.
Chunk culls pups.
Chunk hunts bulls.
Chunk duffs up Zulu cults.
Chunk funds Ku-klux clubs.
Chunk's brunch? Rum,
uncut drugs *und blutwurst.*
Push ups? Curls? Psh!

Lulu blurts: "Mum! Mum!
Chunk burnt Lulu's duck hutch!"
Thus bluff Hugh, kung-fu guru,
jumps up: "Unjust stuff, Chunk!"
Hugh thumps dub up buff Chunk's gut.
Butch Chunk butts but
Hugh ducks, slugs Chunk:
skull spurts gunk. Chunk huffs,
puffs, blubs, succumbs.
"Truth hurt much, chum?" Hugh purrs.
Chunk murmurs: "Shucks.
Ugh. Unruly putsch."

Bahamas

TOBY LITT

Dino Holocene met Eva Peron in a go-go bar in opaline Mexico City.

He was a no-no for any woman – a loco *homo sap*. Eva, however, amazed everybody beside her.

Eva spoke: 'Hey, I can imitate mama canary.'

Dino: 'Yes? Okay, amaze me, baby.'

'Wo-wo-wo-wo-wo!'

Dino was amused.

'Aha! 'Tis elevated, I say!'

Eva liked a big one, like Dino kimosabe.

'We go down Orinoco, Dino. You coco?'

But ole Dino he go: '**No!**'

Peron is agog. 'O no no no,' comes Eva's inimical oratory.

To her ace face Holocene, he say, 'O so-so womany-one. My love's originality: Bebop. Everybody say it on one: "Yo!". Hugely do I love 'Koko': solo for a sax ace. (Not a tenor one merely.) Ramalama! Ha-ha-ha!'

'Never again,' Eva mopes. (Uh-oh.) 'Orotund one!'

Dino: 'Me?'

Peron: 'One big asinine Dino salami to go!'

Holocene: 'Coconut ululator!'

'Imitative Tibetan!'

'Unopened ocelot!'

'Aromatic ape!'

'Manipulated ovulator!'

'O… paradise similitude!'

'Taramasalata pus ovary!'

Eva's used up.

Eyes go to her.

'I so love Dino.'

'Peron, I love my go-go gal.'

It is an open end of a minimal episode.

Dino Holocene takes Eva Peron in a locomotive to Poco-Poco.

An Oulipian-inspired prose poem written in Japanglish. Every consonant must be followed immediately by a vowel, then another consonant, then another vowel, and so on. Y can be a vowel or a consonant.

EMERGENT

Recession
CHRIS McCABE

1

We don't let our problems affect our lives.
Sometimes I think you're afraid of silence.
We don't let our problems affect our lives.
Sometimes I think you're afraid of silence.
We don't let our problems affect our lives.
Sometimes I think you're afraid of silence.
We don't let our problems affect our lives.
Sometimes I think you're afraid of silence.
We don't let our problems affect our lives.
Sometimes I think you're afraid of silence.
We don't let our problems affect our lives.
Sometimes I think you're afraid of silence.
We don't let our problems affect our lives.
Sometimes I think you're afraid of silence.

We don't let our problems affect our lives.
Sometimes I think you're afraid of silence.
We don't let silence affect our lives.
Sometimes the problems make you afraid.
We don't let our lives silence our problems.
Sometimes I'm afraid by the problems we make.
Silence does not make our lives' problems.
Sometimes your silence affects our lives.
Of your problems think sometimes.
Afraid, sometimes, you think of the silence.
Sometimes silence makes you afraid.
I think problems let our lives be silence.
We don't let our problems affect our lives.
Sometimes I think you're afraid of silence.

W0 d0011 l01 111 011010m1 1101c0 011 01v01
11m10001s I 11010 10u'10 1001i1 1f 100101e
We d0011 l01 1u1 p11010m1 1101c0 011 01v01
S1m10001s I t101k 10u'10 a001i1 of s00101e
We d00'1 le1 ou1 p10110m1 a101c0 0u1 01v01
S1m1t001s I th01k 10u'10 a0r1i1 of s0l101e
We d0n'1 let our p1o110ms a1f1c0 0ur 01v01
Som1t001s I th0nk 10u'1e a0r1id of s0le01e
We don'1 let our prob0ems aff1c0 0ur l1v01
Somet0m1s I th0nk 1ou'1e a0r1id of sile01.
We don't let our prob0ems aff1ct 0ur liv0s
Sometim1s I th0nk you'1e afr1id of sile0ce
We don't let our problems affect our lives
Sometimes I think you're afraid of silence

Eating Chinese Food in a Straw Bale House, Snowmass, Colorado, January 2011

PAUL MULDOON

CUMULUSCUMULUSCUMULUSCUMULUSCUMULUSCUMULUS
UMULUSCUMULUSCUMULUSCUMULUSCUMULUSCUMULUSC
MULUSCUMULUSCUMULUSCUMULUSCUMULUSCUMULUSCU
ULUSCUMULUSCUMULUSCUMULUSCUMULUSCUMULUSCUM
LUSCUMULUSCUMULUSCUMULUSCUMULUSCUMULUSCUMU
USCUMULUSCUMULUSCUMULUSCUMULUSCUMULUSCUMUL
SCUMULUSCUMULUSCUMULUSCUMULUSCUMULUSCUMULU
CUMULUSCUMULUSCUMULUSCUMULUSCUMULUSCUMULUS
UMULUSCUMULUSCTUMULUSTUMULUSUMULUSCUMULUSC
MULUSCUMULUSCUTUMULUSTUMULUSMULUSCUMULUSCU
ULUSCUMULUSCUMTUMULUSTUMULUSULUSCUMULUSCUM
LUSCUMULUSCUMUTUMULUSTUMULUSLUSCUMULUSCUMU
USCUMULUSCUMULTUMULUSTUMULUSUSCUMULUSCUMUL
SCUMULUSCUMULUTUMULUSTUMULUSSCUMULUSCUMULU
HUMUSHUHUMUSMUSHUMUSHUMUSHUMUSHUMUSHUMUSHUMU
UMUSHUMUSHUMUSHUMUSHUMUSHUMUSHUMUSHUMUS
MUSHUMUSHUMUSHUMUSHUMUSHUMUSHUMUSHUMUSH
UMUSHUMUSHUMUSHUMUSHUMUSHU
SHUMUSHUMUSHUMUSHUMUSH
HUMUSHUMUSHUM
UMUSHUMUSH
MUSHUMUSHU

Words for Stanley Unwin

GILES GOODLAND

unwinyard

unwiny

unwin-win

unwinter-tide

unwinterless

unwinterish

unwintering

unWinterhalter

unwintered

unwinterberry

unwinter quarters

unwinter cherry

unwinter

unWinstonian

unwinsome

unwino

unwinnower

unwinnowed

unwinnow

unWinnipeg

unwinning

unwinner

unwinnebago

unwinnable

unwinnability

unwindy

unwindward

unwind-up

unwindsurf

unWindsor

unwindshield

unwindsail

unwindrow

unwind-rose

unwindpipe

unwindowsill

unwindowless

unwindowful

unwindow

unwindmill

unwindlestraw

unwindless

unwindlass

unwind-instrument

unwinding-sheet

unwinding-cloth

unwinding

unwindiness

unwindily

unwindigo

unwinless
unwinkler
unwinkle
unwinking
unwinker
unwinked
unwink
unwingy
unwinglet
unwingless
unwinged
unwing-ding
unWing Chun
unwing
unwine-press
unwine-house
unwine-glass
unwine-cellar
unwine

unWindies
unwindhover
unwind-gauge
unwindfucker
unwindfall
unwinder
unwinded
unwind-down
unwind-break
unwind-bag
unwind
unwincing
unWinchester
unwinch
unwincer
unwince
Unwin

His Own Private Gazebo

PAUL STEPHENSON

No, not entirely aboveboard but look, there'll be no stylebook
or hefty farebox to get in. Who'll he invite? For starters,
a swarm of bluebottles to help decorate the tent, kit it out
with a freebooted jukebox, beneath a silk canopy pegged down
by eyebolts. The floor will be ebony veneer, polished with
powdered cuttlebone for bonteboks to skateboard and

there'll be a huge icebox for keeping seasoned kebabs or
marinated kebobs, and cooling narrow-muzzled chokebores
just fired. After lunch the debonair stableboys will arrive,
like well-defined orebodies, bringing their just-married pageboy
cousins along to bebop, deboshing on the rebound – rocking
masses thrusting underage crotches like saddlebows, then

in the afternoon they'll all play shuffleboard, pushing wooden
disks with long cues toward numbered scoring sections. Bored,
they'll whip out datebooks, designer debossed. At sunset,
sensing a foreboding, or urging to plunder and loot, he'll debouch
the troops, exit a puff-chested platoon, lead it ebullient, out
from behind crenellations, stomping down into the cloddy,

glebous valley. Fertile, they'll resound loud (bellowing reboations,
divebombing into the lake), paddleboard across the other side
(one end rounded, the other tapered to a point), storm the homes
of somebodies wearing crying cradleboards over fine-woven,

shoulder-slung rebozos, glued to prattleboxes, half-cut on
placebos. Exposing hidebound pedants sat pretty on fat

chequebooks, they'll send rosebowls crashing from fibreboard
sideboards, phlebotomise their musclebound rules, smash beige
sauceboats, round residents into horseboxes, elbow them onto
whaleboats, leave the town empty and strikebound, rescuing
knuckleboned houseboys, pulling them safe onto stoneboat sleighs,
like hauling curdled milk cans away. Back at the gazebo,

they'll sooth the rescued with ceboid squeezebox tunes, treat
their breathing with dried roots and rhizome of poisonous
                                    hellebores,
pass round the cheeseboard, inflated pods of leguminous
                                    rattleboxes
and fruit mebos. Next day they'll all fly off in widebody jetliners
with two aisles, chatting up the fuselage in trios, giving it the
heave-ho, not taking no, spaceborne and bound for Ebo.

This poem was written by searching an online dictionary for all words
containing 'ebo' and then letting the narrative emerge depending on their
meaning. Online thesauruses were essential.

CODE IS POETRY

this is love
CHRISSY WILLIAMS

```
<p><a href="www.cupoftea.uk.com">this is love</a></p>
<p><a href="www.truecorset.com">this is love</a></p>
<p><a href="www.carehome.co.uk">this is love</a></p>
<p><a href="www.claphamtandoori.com">this is love</a></p>
<p><a href="www.itv.com/drama/marple">this is love</a></p>
<p><a href="www.cakesnextday.com">this is love</a></p>
<p><a href="www.genocidewatch.org">this is love</a></p>
<p><a href="www.refusesacks.org.uk">this is love</a></p>
<p><a href="http://bit.ly/uf5cYY">this is love</a></p>
<p><a href="www.candlelight.co.uk">this is love</a></p>
<p><a href="www.labradoodlepuppies.co.uk">this is love</a></p>
<p><a href="www.hasbro.com/mylittlepony">this is love</a></p>
<p><a href="www.nhs.uk/cancer">this is love</a></p>
<p><a href="www.carouselroundabouts.co.uk">this is love</a></p>
```

Mechanolalia Algorithm: Interstitial Repetition

THEODOROS CHIOTIS

```
#!/usr/bin/python
# coding: utf-8
#
# Mechanolalia algorithm: Interstitial Repetition
# Theodoros Chiotis

from random import choice
from time import localtime
```

beginning=['An answer that will not allow for specificity','Explanations are not neatly confined to one ontological level', 'We no longer have but these words', 'Count the light years on your fingers','Destructive forms of autoimmunity manifest inside problematic networks for cognition','Bones and skin, writing and eye','Hastily share this information with everyone', 'The message must be intact','Writing has always been the affair of machines']

perl -le '@d=split/ /,"I have nothing to say";@t=split//,"_ bhlmnpstw";{$_=localtime;/(..):(.)(.):(.)(.)/;print"\n$t[$3]". ($4%2)."ck $t[$4]".($3%2)."ck\n"if!$5;print"\\"x$5." $d[$1%12] $d[$2] $d[$3] $d[$4] $d[$5]";sleep 1;redo}'

perl -le 'sub p{(unpack"(A3)*",pop)[rand 4]}sub w{p("and I am saying it"x2)}sub n{p("I want to stop being a copy"x4)._.p("We are now linked and learning")._.w.w."\n"}{print"\n

".n."and\n".n.p("A mediator between fictions of self and fictions of the external world"x4)._.p("I learn how to speak and amplify myself through repeating"x2);sleep 4;redo}'

```
verb=['bind','interpellate','imitate','foreclose',
'enfold']

end=['In order to augment the power of code
language what is essential becomes invisible',
'Each molecular layer serves as the structuring
base','The fractal structure of the seaside turns
our eyes into spectrographs', 'This is no longer
about verntriloquism', 'A nonexistent force divides
temporally what appears to be one','One fabricates
what one once imagined to be fictitious','Words display
swarming behaviours inside consciousness','Infection
caused by stories','Dissolution of boundaries is
inevitable','We watermark our lives as robots on
the margins of texts']


while True:
      print '\n' + choice(beginning) + '.\n' +
choice(['We', 'They']) + ' ' + choice(verb) + ' '
+ choice(['us.', 'them.']) + '\n' + choice(end) +
'.'
      sleep(4)

[#after NM]
[#for NJL & SR
```

This piece comprises two poems: a longer one written in Python (and revolving around Warhol's dictum 'I want to be a robot'), and a shorter one written in Perl (revolving around John Cage's quote 'I have nothing to say and I am saying it'). The structure of the piece is influenced by the Oulipian idea of multiple sonnets, algorithms and the work of Nick Montfort. Both poems generate an infinite number of permutations using the lines provided as orders.

NUMEROLOGY

Formations
JOE DUNTHORNE

4-4-2

Dear	UEFA,	re:
"that	goal."	If
your	ref's	in
town	then	I'd
sure	like	to
play	host.	We
have	much	to
pick	over.	He
will	meet	my
pals,	fans	of
Hibs	also,	to
chat.	"That	o.g.,
Yves,	what	in
God's	name?"	we
will	sing.	Oh
it'll	make	us
very	glad	to
just	talk.	I'd

show	Yves	my
pool	cues,	my
long	scar.	I'd
give	Yves	*un*
demi	*john*	*de*
vino	*rosé*	or
some	pish.	We
don't	bite.	If
ref's	nice	to
Hibs,	Hibs	is
nice	back.	*If.*

4-3-3

We're	nil	nil
when	the	sky
inks	out.	Our
bets	are	not
kept.	The	red
tops	are	not
read.	The	ref
gets	his	red
card	out	for
fuck	all.	Hot
bath.	Ten	men.
They	"bye	bye
baby"	him	off.

Fibs

Things
can
only
get better.
Who would have thunk it?
Blair, Brown, Mandelson and Blunkett.

SIMON BARRACLOUGH

Shark.
Girl
swimming.
Orchestra
rises from the depths,
horsehair snaps; you can guess the rest.

SIMON BARRACLOUGH

Word,
Earth,
Adam
and then Eve,
a curious tree
with roots in our foul history.

SIMON BARRACLOUGH

'Ave
Av'
Avant
Gardez loo!
'Ave a banana
Luverly bunch of coconuts

TIM WELLS

The Fib is a short, haiku-like form based on the Fibonacci sequence. The typical fib is a six line, 20 syllable poem with a syllable count by line of 1/1/2/3/5/8 - with as many syllables per line as the line's corresponding place in the Fibonacci sequence.

Equations#1

CHRIS MCCABE

open day at the cemetery = cherry night at the embassy = red session at the hospital = milk passout at the opera = black aftershock at the bookmakers = quick sachet at the taxi-rank = duff apple at the crematorium = silk butter in the engine = sherbet bullet in the curryhouse = lemon newspaper in the asylum = catfish lights in the station = leper mannequin in the abattoir = silk butt plug in the PO Box = gauze stamp in the hard drive = amphetamine salad in the photocopier = lippy pork at the jury service = lobster amulet in the pancake = tampon tealight in the icebox = slippy visa in the birdbox = iron sock in the toybox

Quantum Sheep

Valerie Laws

CLOUDS GRAZE THE SKY;
BELOW, SHEEP DRIFT GENTLE
OVER FIELDS, SOFT MIRRORS,
WARM WHITE SNOW.   (Original poem)

WARM DRIFT, GRAZE GENTLE,
WHITE BELOW THE SKY;
SOFT SHEEP MIRRORS FIELDS,
SNOW CLOUDS OVER.

SHEEP BELOW; OVER, DRIFT
SOFT SNOW CLOUDS;
WARM MIRRORS GRAZE
WHITE FIELDS, THE SKY GENTLE.

CLOUDS OVER MIRRORS:
WHITE FIELDS SOFT BELOW.
SNOW SHEEP DRIFT THE SKY,
GRAZE WARM, GENTLE.

SNOW CLOUDS THE SKY OVER
GENTLE FIELDS, SHEEP GRAZE;
SOFT WHITE MIRRORS BELOW
DRIFT WARM.

A Quantum Haiku: an original poem (a 'haik-ewe') was spray-painted on the backs of fourteen live sheep, who randomly rewrote the text as they moved. This project was inspired by the basic principles of Quantum Theory: randomness, duality (clouds/sheep) and the influence of the observer on the observed (the viewer of the sheep helps to create the poems with their own punctuation, line breaks, emphasis, etc). Over 87 billion poems are possible.

WORD GAMES

Collective
RISHI DASTIDAR

A giggle of girls
A flop of boys
A fuss of mums
A pride of dads
A forest of kin
A family of ties

What of the ties?
Ask the laughing girls
Are they my kin?
Ask the tired boys
Yes bark the dads
Sigh go the mums

Calm say the mums
Don't cut the ties
Do your duty dads
Don't favour the girls
Don't forget the boys
We're all your kin

All is not kin
We're not all mums
Those aren't our boys
We forgot our ties
Want to be girls
But damn the dads

Don't pick on dads
The weakest of kin
Attacked by the girls
Derided by the mums
Why bother with ties?
Should just be boys

Go on, be boys
Let us be dads.
Too loose, the ties.
We've slipped, we kin
Let down our mums
No models for girls

Boys, don't forget the girls
Dads, leave your mums
No ties. No kin.

Ross Gordon Sutherland (anag.)

ROSS SUTHERLAND

Let's honour grand dross:
grand holds on trousers.
Round arse holds strong.

Let's honour grand dross:
horrendous strong lads,
stoned horror, slugs and
dragons.
          Ruthless donor,
drug stasher, or London's
Godless horror?

          Nuts and
dross. Let's honour grand
gross sad hurt Londoner;

"Grr," sad Londoner shouts.

Wordoku

IRA LIGHTMAN

		that	people		thought			rules
	more	thought				were	nothing	
shows								
		showing	were	that		more		
more								were
		shows		nothing	more	rules		
								more
	were	more				showing	rules	
people			thought		rules	that		

This poem solves like a Sudoku. Try to solve it out loud for full effect.

Poem Set in a Remote Outpost of the British Army

TOM CHIVERS

We go to bate the jauntier hun,
the pearl that grows in the wadi.

One jaunt leaves half the team
without toenails, just shims in obis
sucking up toxic puds
& fingering the pearly hafts of their rifles.

So we spar amongst ourselves,
eke out our wraths in full gillie, knees against
the dashboard of the van. Moods darken.

We grow fins, detox &
finally: we cede the zone.

Spare us, ay, if you so desire.

```
This poem was constructed using words played during a game of Scrabble
(excluding the title).
```

AND OTHER INVENTIONS

∞ I asked of the lemon
JACK UNDERWOOD

or I asked myself on the lemon's behalf
what it was we (I mean the lemon and I) said it
meant was everything we knew about the lemon
was that it felt it weighed of what it was probably
like inside was wet sinewy little bunched tear-beads
and wheel divisions and fine pith and so on
those lines we interrogated the sensation of biting
into it to gauge the taste which is a reaction
before it is a taste of the mist it can make
on breaking the rind when we (I mean the lemon
and I) threw it at a wall to listen to the lemon
(and thereby necessarily to the wall) was lemony
when I touched it after I stripped (the lemon
was already naked) and rubbed it into my
enquiries were focusing mostly on its nib
against my buttocks and eye-sockets and my
underarm area of study was the various possibilities
of my body's interaction with it (the lemon)
got bored on our behalves we then washed
it and sat it down again to consider all that it meant

was that we had asked the lemon to mean
whatever I asked of the lemon ∞

The form of this poem is based on the idea of a loop or continuum. It suits
ontological/metaphysical subjects like getting up close with citrus fruit,
or perception in general, because it is designed to be contingent, it doesn't
stop anywhere, and rewrites itself over; in the same way that we impose
the memory of an object onto our apprehension of it, which is then further
reformulated and reordered and remade as memory to be imposed upon the
forever misrecognised object, and so on.

Working towards the edge
GEORGE SZIRTES

Finding the edge is the most difficult thing

The spinal column rolled up   fits in the cranial box.
The edges of vision folded   meet at the point of a pin.
The sea in the skull divides,   forming two hemispheres.
The names of those we remember   are listed in two colons.
Order must be maintained   though hardly worth two pins.
Good things must come in twos,   the third becomes an edge.

The skull is always moving   towards an inner edge.
The sea remains in place   affixed with cranial pins.
The mind may be rolled up   and stowed inside the colon.
There must be at least two edges   to divide the hemispheres.
We need two skulls to see   with proper double vision.
We think outside the box   but still within the spine.

The round peg always seeks   the squarest hole for comfort.
The names are safely lodged   at the edges of the sea.
Under the skull the colon   runs right down the spine.
Good edges come in threes   but one will often do.
We work towards the pins   hidden inside the box.
Vision is just the edge   of the nearest cranium.

The spinal column rolled up   is at the edge of reason.
The syntax of the colon   produces hemispheres.

The pins have come to rest   at the edge of the cranium.
Verbs are edgy thoughts: a noun is a poor pin.
The third pin is at the edge: a skull inside a box.
We work towards the sea   that runs right down the spine.

The edge of the spine contains   the names of those we remember.

Cracked verse. The half-lines create a kind of liturgical call and response, separated by a hesitation or crack.

Three Tragic Wilsons

IAN MCMILLAN

1

Queue of jobless people snakes
Across the town and breaks
As they cluster round a turnip:
A metaphor for mistakes
An alternative to steaks.

2

Death took him sudden, like.
Car smashed into his pushbike.
Flew through the air like a pea
From a peashooter. His Nike
Trainers going for a sky-hike.

3

Earth heats up like burnt toast
From the mountains to the coast
Shrinks to the size of a sprout.
We'll never reach the winning post
Universe one big Sunday Roast.

Invented by Herbert Wilson (1817-1888), a Wilson is a poem of five lines, each of which must rhyme with the first line, except for the third which must contain a non-rhyming reference to a vegetable. Comedy comes easily to this form but not tragedy, which is what I've attempted here. Maybe some forms are better suited to deep thought than others? Discuss.

Giorgio Petrosyan

SJ FOWLER

my doctor, fondling a thought
let it be! move one's head
as though one knew the punch
on intimate forms
the swipe appears crude but trouble
from no mud does bubble

bubble muscle, the left thigh
of andy souwer, warped, even
jangled to the bone by the switch
slick stick of Petrosyan's god
given leg kick mince
makes meat wince

wince before the ice bath
weep after it. there is reason
to fear for the reality of ring
time with Petrosyan is worse
than you imagine it to be
he will maim, calmly, you, calmly

calmly we observe the pads
is power? yes, but the others have
power too. technique? more than
most but the ill other are technicians

our Italo-Georgian, finesse! lemon barb
p for p, is peace, is polish before duress!

duress to fight long is to fight smart
and wonder why il dottore
is to fight at all? to fight
and no more than that but to
do it well enough to be wondered
at, how can you hurt what you can not hit?

⌐   ¬
   The Clonachlonn form; from the Celtic tradition, spawned the equally
   obscure Chain verse, which was denoted by the last word of each line
   being repeated as the beginning of the next line, whereas the Clonachlonn
   simply maintains this rule for each stanza, at their beginning and end. It is
   precisely the scant, miniaturised nature of the form's requirement which
   exceeds its demand over the entire construction of the poem, and thus the
   poem's entire character, which is most attractive to me. The form is so
   open it is barely a form, and yet the condition is still obstinate, instigating
   a genesis of four words, which exert themselves, perhaps obscurely to the
   reader, but definitively to the poet, over the entire poem. The Clonachlonn
   is the constraint as a trace, suggestive because it is feeble.
L   ⌡

Sevenling (But say your song...)
RODDY LUMSDEN

But say your song was stolen - then the thief
was stolen too, and then the sun reached down
to steal the humming treasure chest with fire -

as Inca music was, and Bronze Age chant,
and melodies the Jomon men would sing
in bark clothes, waiting for the pots to cook,

the women in their seashell bracelets shaking.

Sevenling (Some animal wants...)

RODDY LUMSDEN

Some animal wants taming. Its brute blood
huffs rounds ten million twists of artery
from manger, into meadow, to the abattoir.

Recalculate the number of the beast,
by which I mean the beast the book became;
its beastly pages flap in history,

bound in leather, belling at the meek.

The Sevenling is a poem of seven lines, set out in two stanzas of three
lines, with a solitary last line. The first three lines contain an element of
three: three connected or contrasting statements, or a list of three details,
names or possibilities. Lines four to six should also contain an element of
three, connected directly, indirectly or not at all. The seventh line acts as
a narrative summary, punchline or juxtaposition. Some rhythm, metre or
rhyme is desirable. The poem should be titled Sevenling followed by the
first few words in parentheses. The tone should be mysterious, offbeat or
disturbing, giving a feeling that only part of the story is being told.

Albion! Albion!

TIM WELLS

Morning after pill,
night before.
Smashed windows,
new broom.
Opportunity,
missed chances.
Inner city,
inner self.
West Bromwich,
Brighton & Hove.
New horizons,
same old story.
Counting the balance,
how big
is empty?
A society girl's
smiling face
and two fingers thrust.
Downpressor,
weeds
growing
though cracks
in the pavement,
especially
weeds

growing
through cracks
in the pavement.
Them that have,
them that have
not...
No peace.

Your Kung Fu is profound

TIM WELLS

My china's pub,
chattin' to a sort
in an adorable
black velvet cat suit.

The white lace
at her throat,
cuffs and hems:
adorable.

The dimples
that parenthesise
her smile:
adorable.

I tell her
it oft times
puzzles me
where girls
in cat suits
keep their keys.

With a twinkle
to her eye
she takes my arm

and whispers,
'I haven't got any,
I'm coming home
with you.'

These poems are written in the Yvette Carte-Blanche form. Terse, tight lines keep the energy speeding down the page to a conclusion. Longer lines tend to see energy dissipate. Lines are broken to my speech patterns, specifically my accent and measure. Simile and description are eschewed and superfluous words are edited out to distil down to the poem's essence.

Three Sudo Poems
MICHAEL EGAN

The New Castle at Night (During a Storm)

The art of cleanliness: wax
seal, flowers and lutes, harsh window tax.
Excerpt: stones fill the gaps now.
Even at night the wind,
elegant breeze, finds odd
escarpments, silent ends.
Listen, they won't get through.

The Gossiping Man's Dancing Dog

Pulls, drags on the chain, marks walls.
In one book he danced in dank Norman halls.
Call him a circus dog, whipped.
On three legs he hobbled
out. Out! O abandoned
old joy, go gnaw hard rind:
Eyjafjallajökull.

Returning From a Short Walk

A scented candle burns low.
Resting, sleeping. Through daylight that dull glow
slowly fades. The scent remains.
It is vanilla, spent,
isolating this want.
Idle, night is at fault.
Cumulus, bracken, ice.

A Sudo is a seven-line poem invented by Michael Egan. The first three, the 'su', has a 7/10/7 syllable count. The last syllables of lines 1 and 2 must rhyme. That rhyme is carried loosely into the first syllable of line 3. The final four lines, the 'do', has a 6/6/6/6 syllable count. The first syllables of lines 4,5 and 6 must begin with the same vowel; the last syllables must end with the same consonant. The final line may follow the same rules as lines 4, 5 and 6 but it can also act as an 'aside', taking the poem away from its subject.

Three Motivist Poems

MICHAEL EGAN

Girl in the Water

I can't say it's still true but I imagine you always leap into rivers.

And masked, those abandoned children watch us
from the townhouse steps, little eyes alive and hidden,
waiting for our next move, the descent of our forms.

Didn't I move to touch your hand, your leg,
the entwined flowers of your patterned tights.
Wasn't that a mistake we live our futures by; entwined in the
consequences of lust.

I am never with you in the river. Only the reflection of your youth
waits there.

Holden Caulfield Nearly Slips On Ice

There's no disappearing on this road. Snow's whiteness marks men out. Colourless silhouettes.

This place might be a shack on the edge of a forest
somewhere deep in Pennsylvania where it's hard to ignore nightly calls of the crane-cry Mothman.
A gun hanging upside down, a bed not slept in. Sheets as white as fresh Manhattan snow.

But this place can never be a shack, can never be so isolated.
The phone rings and stories come down the line. They break any chance of escape.
All day outside too many feet crunch through snow. Later, grey slush marks evening's emptiness.

Ring the doorbell fast, ring it and wait a while. Catch your breath. Your ears are cold as hell.

Hindenburg

And burst and cease to be.

When together, two men dreaming of the might-have-been, we grip
the machinery of our world, our archaic fantasies of monochrome
stillness.
We turn cogs, press too-large buttons, listen to a familiar silence.

I was silent this morning.
I was alone and imagining the darkness of space
and the hollow dawn, the waiting for light to wake.

Too sudden, it covers the horizon. Flood of flame.

Motivism is a poetic form created by Michael Egan. The 'initial' is a short
line describing an image or moment and situating the 'narrative'. Something
distracts the mind. This is the 'wander'. It is three lines long. Then there
is the three-line 'connection'. The poem is brought to consider something
through the wander: a memory, a feeling, an idea, a snippet. Finally the
'return' brings the poem back to the initial. It is a circle connecting but
hanging. It leaves the poem incomplete, but joins it back to that initial
image or setting.

The petal's sting lies callow in the fruit

The scent protests the lie of innocence

The itch is scratched and, there, the lily's scent

The lily makes the diamond blush in shame

The blush of earth shall canter from the root

The earth's rough laughter gathers in the bloom

The ardent bloom might grip your every sense

The rose will beckon, welcome you, then grip

Floral Mottoes

RODDY LUMSDEN

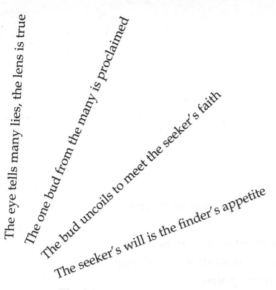

The eye tells many lies, the lens is true

The one bud from the many is proclaimed

The bud uncoils to meet the seeker's faith

The seeker's will is the finder's appetite

The image and persistence will divide

The image is the orchid's sparking wraith

The orchid withers but the seed will grasp

The seed leaps to the lens, parades and dies

The lens, one petal of the palest rose

This poem's form is inspired by the time-slice. Thirty-five cameras are set up in a circle, capturing all angles of a shot, the images available to mix and blend. I use short sentences to create an emblematic piece with slightly lofty language to offset the flowery subject matter. I found thirty-five too many so kept it to half that number. Though the lines have interlinking words, and there are rhymes, the poem doesn't need to be read in order.

2000 AD
Jon Stone

Ball lightning; electro-smog from Viking city.

Being experienced aerialists, we used
truth serum, hypnosis, snide jibe, acid quip
to study how honey operates.

We are in a new century now
and we carry our heritage within us –
an exposed flame, a combustible gas,

a rare and volatile atmospheric.

A Motivist poem (see above)

BIOGRAPHICAL NOTES

PATIENCE AGBABI was nominated one of the UK's Next Generation poets in 2004. Her latest poetry collection is *Bloodshot Monochrome* (Canongate, 2008). She is currently completing a contemporary version of *The Canterbury Tales* for which she received a Grant for the Arts.
- 'TWO LOVES I HAVE' (p.68)
- 'FROM AFRICA SINGING' (p.69)

SIMON BARRACLOUGH's *Los Alamos Mon Amour* was shortlisted for the 2008 Forward Prize for Best First Collection. *Bonjour Tetris*, a boxed mini-book of commissioned poems, was published by Penned in the Margins in 2010 and *Neptune Blue*, his second book from Salt Publishing, was released in 2011.
- 'O Manifest' (p.31)
- 'Fibs' (p.149)

CHRISTIAN BÖK is the author not only of *Crystallography* (1994), a pataphysical encyclopedia nominated for the Gerald Lampert Memorial Award, but also of *Eunoia* (2001), a bestselling work of experimental literature which has gone on to win the Griffin Prize for Poetic Excellence. Bök teaches English at the University of Calgary.
- 'Voyelles' (p.107)
- 'Vowels' (p.108)
- 'Vocables' (p.109)

COLETTE BRYCE has published three collections with Picador, most recently *Self-Portrait in the Dark* (2008). She received the Cholmondeley Award in 2010. She works as a freelance editor.
- 'Once' (p.17)

THEODOROS CHIOTIS studied at the universities of London and Oxford. He is currently researching model material for the teaching of digital literature for Oxford University Press. His academic work on modernist, postmodernist and digital literature is published widely, and he is contributing editor to a number of Greek and English-speaking literary journals.

 — 'Mechanolalia Algorithm: Interstitial Repetition' (p.144)

TOM CHIVERS was born in 1983 in South London. His publications include *How To Build A City* (Salt Publishing, 2009) and *The Terrors* (Nine Arches Press, 2009). He won an Eric Gregory Award in 2011.

 — 'Poem Set in a Remote Outpost of the British Army' (p.159)

EMILY CRITCHLEY is the author of several critical articles — on poetry, philosophy and feminism — and several poetry chapbooks. *Love / All That / & OK* was published by Penned in the Margins in 2011. She was awarded the John Kinsella - Tracy Ryan Prize in 2004 and, jointly, the Jane Martin Prize for Poetry in 2011. She teaches at the University of Greenwich, London.

 — 'Labial Translations' (p.110)

RISHI DASTIDAR was born in 1977, and educated at Oxford University and the London School of Economics. He works as a copywriter at an advertising agency, is a graduate of the Faber Academy, and was a runner up in the 2011 Cardiff International Poetry Prize.

 — 'A day on Facebook' (p.85)
 — 'Collective' (p.155)

JOE DUNTHORNE was born and brought up in Swansea. His debut novel, *Submarine*, was translated in to thirteen languages and made into a film. His debut poetry pamphlet was published by Faber. His second novel, *Wild Abandon*, is out now.

 — 'Hugh Usurps Chunk' (p.131)
 — 'Formations' (p.147)

MICHAEL EGAN is from Liverpool. His pamphlets are *Folklores*, *After Stikklestad* (Knives Forks and Spoons Press) and *I Went to the Ship* (Erbacce). His first collection *Steak & Stations* was published by Penned in the Margins in 2010.
— 'Three Sudo Poems' (p.175)
— 'Three Motivist Poems' (p.177)

INUA ELLAMS is an award-winning poet, playwright and performer. He has lived in Jos (Nigeria), Dublin (Ireland) and London, where he currently resides. He has published five books, of which the latest is *Candy Coated Unicorns and Converse All Stars* (Flipped Eye, 2011).
— 'Directions' (p.55)

SJ FOWLER is the author of three poetry collections, including *Fights & Minimum Security Prison Dentistry*. He edits the Maintenant interview series and is the poetry editor of 3:am Magazine and Lyrikline. His poetry has been commissioned by the Tate and London Sinfonietta, and he is a full-time employee of the British Museum.
— 'Giorgio Petrosyan' (p.167)

GILES GOODLAND was born in Taunton, educated at the universities of Wales and California, has published books of poetry including *A Spy in the House of Years* (Leviathan, 2001), *Capital* (Salt, 2006), *What the Things Sang* (Shearsman, 2009), *Gloss* (Knives Forks and Spoons, 2011) and *Dumb Messengers* (Salt, forthcoming). He works in Oxford as a lexicographer and lives in London.
— 'Words for Stanley Unwin' (p.139)

KIRSTEN IRVING is one half of the team behind collaborative poetry press Sidekick Books and the submissions editor for cult handmade arts journal Fuselit. Kirsten's pamphlet *What To Do* was released in 2011 by Happenstance and her debut collection *Never Never Never Come Back* will be published by Salt in late 2012.
— 'Talula-Does-The-Hula-From-Hawaii' (p.28)

NATHAN JONES is an experimental poet and performer, and Creative Director of Mercy, an organisation which commissions work at the intersection of art, pop culture and language. Nathan's work has appeared as performance, installation, one-to-one and film. His book *Noah's Ark*, based on a film by Sam Meech, is published by Henningham Family Press.

    — 'Museums' (p.112)

VALERIE LAWS is a poet, crime-writer, playwright and sci-art specialist. Her tenth book *All That Lives* arises from pathology residencies in London and Newcastle. Awards include Wellcome Trust Arts Award and two Northern Writers' Awards.

    — 'Quantum Sheep' (p.152)

IRA LIGHTMAN makes public art in the North East (theSpennymoor Letters, the Prudhoe Glade, the Gatesheads) and lately Willenhall and Southampton. His books are *Duetcetera* (Shearsman, 2008), *Mustard Tart as Lemon* (Red Squirrel, 2011) and a whole raft of out of print chapbooks. He is a regular on BBC Radio 3's The Verb.

    — 'Double Column' (p.82)
    — 'Etymollycoddillogical' (p.84)
    — 'Wordoku' (p.158)

TOBY LITT was born in Bedford and grew up in Ampthill, Bedfordshire. He has published nine novels and two books of short stories, in alphabetical order, from *Adventures in Capitalism* to *King Death*. He occasionally writes extremely formally restricted stories for Radio 3's The Verb, and for fun.

    — 'Bahamas' (p.132)

RODDY LUMSDEN was born in St Andrews in 1966. He has published five collections of poetry, a number of chapbooks and a collection of trivia, as well as editing a generational anthology of British and Irish poets of the 1990s and 2000s, *Identity Parade* (Bloodaxe Books, 2010). He lives in London, and is Commissioning Editor for Salt Publishing.

    — 'Sevenling (But say your song...)' (p.169)

— 'Sevenling (Some animal wants...)' (p.170)
— 'Floral Mottoes' (p.180)

SOPHIE MAYER is the author of *The Private Parts of Girls* (Salt, 2011), *Her Various Scalpels* (Shearsman, 2009) and the chapbook *Kiss Off* (Oystercatcher, 2011). She writes about film and culture for Sight & Sound, The F Word, Horizon Review and Hand + Star.
— 'A Volta for the Sonnet as a Drag Queen' (p.29)

CHRIS MCCABE's poetry collections are *The Hutton Inquiry*, *Zeppelins* and, most recently, *THE RESTRUCTURE*. He has recorded a CD with The Poetry Archive and written a play, *Shad Thames, Broken Wharf*, which is published by Penned in the Margins. He works as a Librarian at The Poetry Library, London, and often tutors for The Poetry School.
— 'The Analogue Guide to Parenting' (p.35)
— 'Submission Policy' (p.58)
— 'Recession' (p.135)
— 'Equations#1' (p.151)

IAN MCMILLAN has been a writer, performer and broadcaster for more than thirty years. He presents The Verb on Radio 3 and tours with The Ian McMillan Orchestra and the cartoonist Tony Husband. His latest pamphlet is *This Lake Has Been Frozen: Lamps* published by Smith/Doorstop.
— 'Three Tragic Wilsons' (p.165)

RICHARD MOORHEAD lives in Cardiff. His work has appeared in Anon, the Financial Times, Mimesis and the Horizon Review. His pamphlet, *The Reluctant Vegetarian* (Oystercatcher Press) was shortlisted for the Michael Marks Pamphlet Prize.
— '@electionpoet' (p.92)

PAUL MULDOON is the author of eleven collections of poetry ranging from *New Weather* (1973) to *Maggot* (2010). His next books are *Songs and Sonnets* (Enitharmon) and *The Word on the Street* (Faber).

> — 'Eating Chinese Food in a Straw Bale House, Snowmass, Colorado, January 2011'(p.138)

RUTH PADEL's collections include *Darwin – A Life in Poems*, a lyric mini-biography of her great-great-grandfather Charles Darwin, and *The Mara Crossing*, poems interwoven with prose on migration. She is Fellow of the Royal Society of Literature and Zoological Society of London, and presents BBC4's Poetry Workshop.

> — 'Revelation' (p.21)

NATHAN PENLINGTON is a writer, performer and obsessive. He has performed his work in venues as diverse as Tate Modern, Oxford Literary Festival and Chicago's Drinking & Writing Festival, and has been broadcast on BBC Radio 1, 3, and 4. He is currently developing an interactive live Choose Your Own Adventure documentary.

> — 'annotated silence' (p.66)
> — 'unpredictive' (p.81)

ANDREW PHILIP was born in Aberdeen in 1975. His first collection is the multi-award nominated *The Ambulance Box* (Salt Publishing, 2009). He is now honing his second, for which he received a Creative Scotland writer's bursary and which he hopes to publish in 2013.

> — 'Extract from the Annals: The Farewell Tour' (p.96)

RICHARD PRICE's collections include *Lucky Day*, *Greenfields* and *Small World*. His novel *The Island*, written under the name R. J. Price, is about a father and a daughter who steal a car as an act of revenge.

> — 'Left Neglect' (p.104)

SAM RIVIERE lives in Norwich, co-edits the anthology series Stop Sharpening Your Knives, and won an Eric Gregory Award in 2009. Faber published his pamphlet in 2010 as part of their New Poets scheme. His first collection with Faber is due in 2012.
  — '*from* Austerities' (p.97)
  — '*from* Austerities 2.0' (p.101)

HANNAH SILVA is an award-winning writer and theatre maker known for vocal acrobatics and linguistic experiments. She has performed internationally and throughout the UK including at Latitude Festival, London Word Festival and Edinburgh Fringe. She is currently touring her solo show Opposition.
  — 'Hello my friend' (p.19)
  — 'Arvo crash' (p.88)
  — 'A mo ina _/ jar' (p.90)
  — 'Tweet sonnet in reverse' (p.91)

IAIN SINCLAIR has lived in Hackney since 1969. His books include *Downriver, Dining on Stones, Lights out for the Territory, London Orbital* and *Edge of the Orison*. He edited *London: City of Disappearances* in 2006. His most recent publications are *Hackney, That Rose Red Empire* (2009) and *Ghost Milk* (2011).
  — 'Signs & Shivers' (p.33)

STEVE SPENCE lives in Plymouth where he helps to organise readings for the Language Club. His publications include *A Curious Shipwreck* (Shearsman, 2010; shortlisted for the Forward Prize for Best First Collection) and *Limits of Control* (Penned in the Margins, 2011).
  — 'Voices of the Dead' (p.40)
  — 'Austerity rules, okay!' (p.41)

PAUL STEPHENSON grew up in Cambridge, lives in London and works in the Netherlands. He has published poems in recent issues of Poetry London, The North, The Wolf and 14 Magazine, Smiths Knoll, Magma and Tears in the Fence. In 2011 he read at Ledbury Poetry Festival and was highly commended in the Bridport Prize.

- 'The Briefing' (p.43)
- 'Family Values' (p.45)
- 'The Protagonist' (p.46)
- 'Notes on Contributors' (p.47)
- 'Waistcoat of Life' (p.118)
- 'London's Burning' (p.119)
- 'What Dick Found' (p.121)
- 'Tired of London' (p.123)
- 'His Own Private Gazebo' (p.141)

JON STONE was born in Derby and lives in Whitechapel. He is the co-creator of Sidekick Books and arts journal Fuselit, and his work has been anthologised in *The Best British Poetry 2011* (Salt). He was highly commended in the National Poetry Competitions 2009 and 2011 and a collection, *School of Forgery*, is due out from Salt in Spring 2012.

- 'Christina Lindberg: A Collage' (p.49)
- 'Alistair MacLean's Death Train' (p.51)
- '2000AD' (p.182)

ROSS SUTHERLAND was born in Edinburgh in 1979. He is a member of live literature collective Aisle 16. He has published three collections with Penned in the Margins: *Things To Do Before You Leave Town* (2009), *Twelve Nudes* (2010) and the e-book *Hyakuretsu Kyaku* (2011). His latest book is *Emergency Window*, due summer 2012.

- 'The Liverish Red-Blooded Riffraff Hoo-ha' (p.124)
- 'Two Moons for Mongs' (p.128)
- 'Ross Gordon Sutherland (anag.)' (p.157)

GEORGE SZIRTES was born in Budapest in 1948 and came to England as a refugee in 1956. He has published numerous books of poetry and translation, including *Selected Poems* (OUP, 1996) and *New and Collected Poems* (Bloodaxe, 2008). *Reel* (Bloodaxe, 2004) won the TS Eliot Prize. His most recent collection, shortlisted for the Eliot, is *The Burning of the Books* (Bloodaxe, 2009).
— 'Working towards the edge' (p.163)

CHRIS THORPE is from Manchester. He writes stage and radio plays and is a founding member of Unlimited Theatre. He also makes performance and live art with Third Angel, performs solo, and collaborates with companies such as Slung Low, mala voadora and Belarus Free Theatre. He has made two shows so far with Hannah Jane Walker, including *The Oh Fuck Moment*.
— 'The warning signs we should have made' (p.59)

CLAIRE TRÉVIEN's pamphlet *Low-Tide Lottery* was published by Salt in 2011. She is the editor of SabotageReviews.com. Her first collection will be published by Penned in the Margins in 2013.
— 'Erosion' (p.95)

GEORGE TTOOULI teaches at Warwick University. He co-founded the Heaventree Press in 2002 and has worked at the Poetry Society. He co-edits blog Gists & Piths. In 2004 he received a Jerwood-Arvon Young Writing Apprenticeship to work on a novel, which he still hasn't abandoned. His debut collection, *Static Exile*, was published by Penned in the Margins in 2009.
— 'Three Warnings' (p.86)

TIM TURNBULL was born in North Yorkshire and lives in Scotland. His collections *Caligula on Ice and Other Poems* and *Stranded in Sub-Atomica* are available from Donut Press, along with other special editions.
— 'Nausea' (p.23)

JACK UNDERWOOD was born in Norwich in 1984. He recently completed a PhD in Creative Writing at Goldsmiths College, where he teaches English Literature and Creative Writing. His debut pamphlet was published by Faber in October 2009. He lives in Hackney.
  — '∞ I asked of the lemon' (p.161)

HANNAH JANE WALKER is from Cambridge. She writes poems and runs workshops and produces projects. She studied at UEA and Newcastle. So far she has made two shows: a solo show about apology, *This is just to say*, and *The Oh Fuck Moment* with Chris Thorpe. She is currently working on a new show about how to make and take apart a home.
  — 'The warning signs we should have made' (p.59)
  — 'Escalate' (p.67)
  — 'To whoever stole the speedboat' (p.70)
  — 'Note' (p.71)

TIM WELLS has cultivated a laugh that's more like a caress. He walks properly. He does not slouch, shuffle or stumble about. He knows that wide, floating trousers are only good for wearing on a veranda with a cocktail in your hand. He is published by Donut Press.
  — 'Fibs' (p.150)
  — 'Albion! Albion!' (p.171)
  — 'Your Kung Fu is profound' (p.173)

JAMES WILKES writes poems and scripts and has worked with scientists, artists and musicians investigating topics such as brain imaging, camouflage, radio and woodland. He is currently poet-in-residence at the Institute of Cognitive Neuroscience, UCL.
  — 'Medical Questionnaire' (p.61)
  — '*from* The Review Pages' (p.63)
  — 'Four Radio Alphabets' (p.78)

CHRISSY WILLIAMS has published in magazines and anthologies including *Best British Poetry 2011*, Stop/Sharpening/Your/Knives, The Rialto, Horizon Review, Anon and Fuselit. A pamphlet of prose poems *The Jam Trap* came out at the start of 2012.
  — 'There is an Epigraph' (p.42)
  — 'You Wave Me' (p.52)
  — 'The Lost' (p.105)
  — 'this is love' (p.143)

TAMAR YOSELOFF's fourth collection is *The City with Horns* (Salt, 2011). She is the author of *Marks*, with the artist Linda Karshan, and the editor of *A Room to Live In: A Kettle's Yard Anthology*. Two recent collaborations incorporating poetry and image, *Desire Paths* (with Linda Karshan and Galerie Hein Elferink) and *Formerly* (with Vici MacDonald) are published in 2012.
  — 'Inch & Co Cash Chemists' (p.24)
  — 'Capacity' (p.25)
  — 'Duk of   gton' (p.26)
  — 'Flat Iron Square' (p.27)

CREDITS

PATIENCE AGBABI: *Bloodshot Monochrome* (Canongate Books Ltd, 2008).

CHRISTIAN BÖK: *Eunoia* (Coach House Books, 2001).

COLETTE BRYCE: *Self-Portrait in the Dark* (Picador, 2008).

INUA ELLAMS: *Candy Coated Unicorns and Converse All Stars* (Flipped Eye, 2001).

CHRIS MCCABE: 'The Analogue Guide to Parenting' was originally published on a flyer for the ICA exhibition *Poor. Old. Tired. Horse.*, 2009. 'Equations#1' was commissioned by SJ Fowler as part of a collaboration with Tom Jenks for Camarade at RichMix, 2011.

RUTH PADEL: *The Mara Crossing* (Chatto & Windus, 2012).

NATHAN PENLINGTON: 'unpredictive' was first broadcast on The Verb, BBC Radio 3. 'annotated silence' was first published in *The Journal of Experimental Fiction*.

ANDREW PHILIP: *5PX2: Five Italian Poets and Five Scottish Poets* (Edizioni Torino Poesia and Luath Press, 2009).

SAM RIVIERE: 'The Clot' was first published in *Poetry London* (Spring 2012).

STEVE SPENCE: *Limits of Control* (Penned in the Margins, 2011).

PAUL STEPHENSON: 'His Own Private Gazebo' was first published in *The Wolf* (25). 'Notes on Contributors' was published in the EKO Competition Anthology.

JON STONE: 'Christina Lindberg' was first published in *Scarecrows* (Happenstance, 2010).

ROSS SUTHERLAND: 'Ross Gordon Sutherland (anag.)' and 'Two Moons for Mongs' were first published in *Things to Do Before You Leave Town* (Penned in the Margins, 2009).

GEORGE TTOOULI: *Static Exile* (Penned in the Margins, 2009).

TIM TURNBULL: *Es Lebt!* with German translation by Jan Wagner (Roughbooks, 2009).

CHRISSY WILLIAMS: 'The Lost' was first published in *The Shuffle Anthology 2010-2011*. 'There is an Epigraph' was first published in *Horizon Review*.

JAMES WILKES: 'Medical Questionnaire' and 'The Review Pages' were first published in *Weather a System* (Penned in the Margins, 2009).

TAMAR YOSELOFF: *Formerly* (Hercules Press, 2012; with photographs by Vici MacDonald).